In our time, which presents a rare phenomenon in the history of the Church—where high ecclesiastical authorities are demanding obedience from priests and faithful in order to force them to collaborate in the process of weakening the integrity of the Faith and of the Sacred Liturgy—the present book of Dr. Peter Kwasniewski offers a valuable and timely theological clarification on the authentic meaning of obedience. This tract will bring peace of conscience to many perplexed souls and confirm their fidelity to the perennial doctrinal and liturgical tradition of Holy Mother Church.

—**Most Rev. Athanasius Schneider**
Auxiliary Bishop of the
Archdiocese of Saint Mary in Astana

We live in unprecedented times, not seen since the Crucifixion of Christ. Divine Providence has determined that each of us should live in such times, as the Church undergoes its own Passion as the Mystical Christ. How are we to discern between obedience to God and obedience to men, when those in ecclesiastical authority refuse subservience to God and have forfeited our trust? This wonderful tract provides solid principles for our discernment, especially relevant in the face of new assaults upon Catholic tradition, and it will strengthen our resolve to obey God in all things.

—**Fr. John Paul Echert, SSL**
Biblical Institute

T0021287

Our loving and gentle Savior spoke these words to the religious leaders of His day: "Woe to you, scribes and Pharisees, hypocrites! because you shut the kingdom of heaven against men; for you neither enter yourselves, nor allow those who would enter to go in. Woe to you, scribes and Pharisees, hypocrites! for you traverse sea and land to make a single proselyte, and when he becomes a proselyte, you make him twice as much a child of hell as yourselves" (Mt 23:13–13). Dr. Kwasniewski, for the love of Truth, has written this tract in the spirit of Truth Himself, for love of God and of His Church. I am exceedingly grateful that such a son of the Church would assist us at this most difficult time to know how to respond to the many false and unreasonable dictates of a number of Her hierarchy. I consider *True Obedience in the Church* to be not only a must-read, but a healing balm of clarity for the Faithful.

> **—Mother Miriam of the Lamb of God, O.S.B.**
> **Host of *Mother Miriam Live!* and Foundress of**
> **the Daughters of Mary, Mother of Israel's Hope**

This is the kind of work I have come to expect from Dr. Kwasniewski: Careful, thoughtful, rigorous, scholarly yet accessible, and worthy of further consideration, prayer, and action. Please take the time to read this work closely and share it with others. It can be the beginning of a longer conversation that faithful Catholics urgently need to have.

> **—Fr. Robert McTeigue, S.J., Ph.D.**
> **Author of *Real Philosophy for Real People*:**
> ***Tools for Truthful Living* and host of *The Catholic Current***

When it comes to obedience, human beings are prone to fall into one of two opposite errors: to obey only when they feel like it (or when constrained by immediate sanctions), or to give to some man an obedience that is due only to God. How can we avoid both these vices? Following the teaching of St. Thomas Aquinas, Peter Kwasniewski puts forward timeless principles that can help us navigate the strait of true obedience in difficult times.

—**Fr. Thomas Crean, O.P.**
Author of *The Mass and the Saints*

As a student of St. John Henry Newman, I was delighted to hear that Dr. Kwasniewski was writing his own "tract for the times," expanding on the excellent talk he gave at the Catholic Identity Conference. As a canceled priest myself, I jumped out of my seat clapping when the good doctor finished his CIC talk. To explain so succinctly the limits of obedience brings solace to canceled priests who are often jeered for "not being obedient." One line echoed in my ears: "Take away truth, and you take away love; take away love, and you take away the root of obedience." I highly recommend this work for both clergy and laity.

—**Fr. John P. Lovell**
Co-founder, The Coalition for Canceled Priests

As an elderly former Anglican cleric and now a Catholic priest, I find the attack on the authentic use of the Roman Rite, implicit in Pope Francis's *Traditionis Custodes*, bewildering. Back in the 1960s when I was ordained, the finest Anglican liturgical scholars had reached a consensus that the Roman Canon was a gift through Holy Tradition from the Church's early centuries. Its replacement was deemed inconceivable. Not even a pope could lawfully tamper with it. Professor Kwasniewski demonstrates with scrupulous care the obligation laid upon us by God to obey Him over any man whose will leads us from Him, be it even a pope. His exposition of Catholic teaching on obedience is a fine and lucid account which, I am sure, will help and encourage many, clergy and laity, who are troubled by the present situation in the Catholic Church.

—Fr. John Hunwicke

True Obedience in the Church

A Guide to Discernment in Challenging Times

Related books by Peter Kwasniewski

Resurgent in the Midst of Crisis
Noble Beauty, Transcendent Holiness
Tradition and Sanity
Reclaiming Our Roman Catholic Birthright
The Holy Bread of Eternal Life
Ministers of Christ
A Reader in Catholic Social Teaching
Newman on Worship, Reverence, and Ritual
And Rightly So: Selected Letters and Articles of Neil McCaffrey
Are Canonizations Infallible?
From Benedict's Peace to Francis's War

Peter Kwasniewski

True Obedience in the Church

A Guide to Discernment
in Challenging Times

SOPHIA INSTITUTE PRESS
Manchester, New Hampshire

Sophia Institute Press
Box 5284, Manchester, NH 03108
1-800-888-9344

www.SophiaInstitute.com

Sophia Institute Press® is a registered trademark of Sophia Institute.

paperback ISBN 978-1-64413-674-4

ebook ISBN 978-1-64413-675-1

Library of Congress Control Number: 2021950932

First printing

"Until the final climax saints may arise and, using their freedom rightly, steer their generations toward the true light, for the good of many souls."

"And by implication, those who govern wisely might also arise."

"It is possible, if there is conversion of heart. Yet the heart alone is not enough. There must be radiant truth in the mind, and for this, I believe, an illumination of conscience is necessary."

—Michael O'Brien, dialogue from *The Sabbatical*

True obedience is the obedience of a person who, in obeying, is able to rise to and unite his will with that of God. False obedience is that of a person who divinizes the man who represents authority and accepts unlawful orders from him.

—Roberto de Mattei

Contents

Preface

An earlier version of this text was given as a lecture at the Catholic Identity Conference in Pittsburgh on October 2, 2021. It has been considerably expanded for publication. I have chosen endnotes rather than footnotes to make for an uncluttered layout and for smooth sailing, as some readers might prefer, on a first reading, to skip the notes in order to stay focused on the main argument. I would, however, encourage such readers to circle back and make a study of the extensive notes, which develop points made in the main text and support them with references. To avoid the unsightly clutter of hyperlinks, most internet sources have been referred to very simply by author, title of piece, title of website, and date; an online search will turn them up in a split second. The section "Further Reading" provides a narrative bibliography for those who wish to delve deeper into the many issues raised in these pages.

I would like to express my thanks to the team at Sophia Institute Press who encouraged me to publish this tract and who saw it quickly through production; to several priests and laymen who took the time to read various iterations of the text and offered many helpful suggestions; and lastly, to the many faithful Catholics who are prepared to "fight the good fight" of preserving and passing on Catholic Tradition, come what may. Like our traditional worship, our obedience too should be rendered "in spirit and in truth," with firm faith, right reason, and a clean conscience.

True Obedience in the Church
A Guide to Discernment in Challenging Times

A friend once told me the story of how, when he was a graduate student at Harvard Divinity School, he went before the faculty to present his idea for a doctoral thesis: the obedience of Jesus in the Gospel of John. There was a moment's pause, and one of the senior professors, a famous liberal, leaned forward and said: "This is an unacceptable topic. Obedience is the root of all evils."

This senior professor was a German who had lived through the horrors of National Socialism, when millions of citizens suppressed the voice of their consciences and followed a crazed dictator into horrific disaster, in the name of obedience to leader, people, and nation. The professor's attitude was for that reason understandable. The same attitude is understandable today in the Catholic Church, when the unveiling of the corruption of prelates at all levels coupled with a pattern of abusive exercise of power prompts the faithful to withhold not only funding but also moral cooperation and intellectual assent. "Obedience to *them*? Are you kidding?" might become a common refrain.

> If we understand how both conscience
> and virtue operate, we will see that
> there can be no such thing as "blind
> obedience" in the Christian life.

Obedience often has a bad name because of authority abused and trust misplaced. In the political sphere, authority has too often not been directed to the common good of the people but to the private good of the politicians or special interest groups, a phenomenon that has become rampant in American politics. Something similar can be seen in the manner in which some prelates, religious superiors, or husbands and fathers have ruled more for their own comfort and convenience than for the genuine good of their subjects. The rise of liberalism (including feminism) is, at least in part, a reaction against real abuses, even as Protestantism, grandfather of modern liberalism, justified its dissent in the face of a late medieval Christendom of appalling moral laxity and religious abuses. Taking all this together with twentieth-century fascism and communism, we are perhaps not surprised by the Harvard professor's generalization, for blind obedience to those who claim power over souls can be a terrible thing.

Obedience as a supreme virtue, modeled by Christ

Yet we must be careful not to throw the baby out with the bathwater. The statement that "obedience is the root of all evils" expresses the very attitude of modernity. The so-called Enlightenment was born out of a desire to be *free from authority*, to "think for oneself" and stand in no relation of dependency on anyone else—to be, in short, the god of one's own world. We find Immanuel Kant saying in his short essay "What Is Enlightenment?"[1] that man can be free only if he is free from everyone and dares to think *by* himself, *for* himself (*aude sapere*); as long as he is dependent on another, he is a slave. Such thoughts flow from the same destructive delusion that fallen man has always entertained after the fatal disobedience of Adam and Eve. Though dressed in the elegant garb of Königsberg, Kant's position differs in no way from that of the serpent in the garden of Eden.

The truth is much different. As St. Thomas Aquinas says in his beautiful work *On the Perfection of the Spiritual Life*,[2] obedience is the proper response of the creature, who is a servant by nature and by grace; it is the path of one who knows his dependence on others for achieving his end, who understands the primacy of his Maker and Lord and trusts in the order established by Divine Providence. By humbly obeying God and His representatives on earth, man negates the illusion of autonomy and enters into the liberty of the children of God who are led by *His* Spirit of love, not by their own easily mistaken desires. In fact, Aquinas says that man makes a *perfect* offering of himself not by giving up external goods, not even by giving up family ties and marriage, but *only* by giving up his own will.

The exemplar of this liberating obedience is Our Lord Himself, about whom St. Paul says:

Let this mind be in you, which was also in Christ Jesus: Who being in the form of God, thought it not robbery to be equal with God: but emptied himself, taking the form of a servant, being made in the likeness of men, and in habit found as a man. He humbled himself, *becoming obedient unto death*, even to the death of the cross. For which cause God also hath exalted him, and hath given him a name which is above all names: that in the name of Jesus every knee should bow, of those that are in heaven, on earth, and under the earth: and that every tongue should confess that the Lord Jesus Christ is in the glory of God the Father. (Phil 2:5–11)

Astonishingly, the Son of God, coequal to the Father and to the Holy Spirit in their one divine nature, nevertheless submitted to the humiliations of our fallen human condition when He hid His glory to take on the form and role of a servant and embraced out of obedience the most humiliating torture and death in order to redeem us from our sins and from the punishments our sins deserved; and He allowed all of this to occur at the hands of the religious and political authorities of His day. In this way Christ took up and divinized our duty of subordination and submission to those placed above us by God; and for it, He was highly exalted.

Our Lord Jesus Christ presents to us the royal road of obedience that has always been put forward by the great saints: by St. Paul in his many letters; by St. Benedict in his *Holy Rule*; by the Desert Fathers and the Fathers of the Church; by Thomas à Kempis in the *Imitation of Christ*; by the Carmelite masters such as St. Teresa of Jesus and St. John of the Cross; and the list goes on.[3] What is more, the traditional liturgical rites of East and West offer us a perfect model and school of obedience because they put forth a complete order of worship, down to every last prayer, chant, and ceremony, and ask the ministers to submit to this order, to put it on the way they put on their vestments, and to obey it so totally that their individuality disappears and the primacy of Christ the Eternal High Priest comes to the fore. The Lord uses His ordained ministers as His animate rational instruments, the way a composer and a conductor employ the musicians in an orchestra to draw forth the beauty of a pre-written musical score.[4] The traditional liturgy exemplifies the virtue of obedience by having the priest obey the rigorous and comprehensive rubrics, giving him no options, no room for spontaneous improvisation, no open-ended flexibility of movement. He humbles himself, takes up the Cross, and follows Christ to Calvary.

Our Lord Jesus Christ presents to us the royal road of obedience that has always been put forward by the great saints.

The structure and strictures of obedience

Having said this, however, we must immediately confront a problem—the very problem that the elderly Harvard professor put his finger on, with awkward exaggeration. Clearly, the obedience of one man to another mere man is not, and can never be, unconditional or, to use the more common language, "blind." So the remainder of this tract will be about the limits of obedience and when it is justified to disobey the command or the ruling of a superior within an earthly hierarchy, including and especially within the Catholic Church.

We must begin by seeing that it is not *obedience* that comes first, but *truth* and *charity*; and this is why obedience, rightly understood, is not blind. In the order of being, there is first the truth, and the love of this truth; and then, obedience is the only appropriate response to truth, the only appropriate response of the will to truth that is to be loved for its own sake. Take away truth, and you take away love; take away love, and you take away the root of obedience.[5] The New Testament insists on obedience to the Lord's commandments as the manifestation of true charity.[6]

Within this Christian life, God places certain obligations on us, according to definite vocations. When a man and woman get married, they accept the duties of their

7

state in life; they need to do whatever God asks them to do as spouses and parents. This is by no means easy, but it is a clear, concrete instance of obedience in action, and the experience of the saints has been that this obedience to one's calling is liberating. The obligations are based on the nature of the state in life: the married have obligations derived from natural law and divine law that they cannot justly shirk. This places God-given limits on, for example, what a husband can require of his wife or what parents can require of their children. The relationship of superior and subordinate always takes place within the context of God's revealed will as authoritatively taught by the Church.

Beyond the duty of our state in life, we are called to give obedience to all legitimate authority derived from God and exercised, at least obliquely, in His name. In the concise affirmation found (in slightly different wording) in countless different Catholic catechisms issued throughout the centuries: "What is commanded by the fourth commandment? To love, honor, and obey parents and superiors.... For there is no power but from God, and those that are, are ordained of God."[7] It is enough to say that the nearer one is to Jesus Himself and His immaculate Bride, the Catholic Church, the more absolute is the obedience owed; the further away, the more qualified and in need of prudential judgment. There will never be a case where the exercise of prudence is not involved at all, at least in the sense of giving us a green light to proceed with whatever course of action has been proposed to us.[8] We have to see, at a minimum, that it does not obviously contradict a good to which we have a prior, more definitive commitment.

> Conscience, therefore, certainly
> does not mean "what I feel
> like doing or not doing."

Catholics owe their superiors in the Church free, intelligent, conscientious obedience. What does that mean? For obedience to be able to be given, there are two fundamental conditions that must always be present, either explicitly or implicitly.

First, there is trust. Trust is based on a belief that the superior loves us with Christian charity and wills our good, or at the very least does not seek our injury or destruction.[9] Little children have this trust quite naturally toward their parents, and in most cases it is fully justified by the affection the parents have for the children. This is why obedience, though difficult for fallen human nature, is natural and obvious enough within the family. But we know, sadly, that in an abusive family, where a child sees that a parent is actually harming or seeking to harm him, trust is undermined, and therefore an essential condition for the child's obedience to the parent vanishes.

Second, there is what might be called *rightful subordination*. This means two things. First, it means that the superior himself is obedient to higher authority. The superior must subject himself to God: to divine law and natural law. But he should also be respectful of custom and tradition, especially within the Church, where these things have the force of law.[10] Second, it means that the inferior is subject to the superior only in those matters over which the superior has discretion or command, and that the inferior has the capacity to see when the superior is or may be transgressing the boundaries of his own position.

God alone, being supremely and infinitely good, being Love itself, deserves absolute and unconditional obedience, because He is worthy of all our trust; He has no superior, but is Himself the source and model and righteousness of all superiors, and He never wills anything other than our good.

A crucial aspect of trust in a superior is having confidence that he is telling the truth. Again, we can normally assume that someone is telling us the truth unless circumstances point strongly to the conclusion that we are being lied to or manipulated. If we have a well-founded suspicion that a superior is lying in any matter that bears on our salvation, we would be justified in having some skepticism toward him and what he is demanding.[11] A related issue is that we should have a basic confidence that the superior is not himself being lied to or manipulated by his own superior or by his counselors. Again, there's no reason to assume this is happening, but there are times when it's clear that someone has been badly or falsely informed. Actions that flow from falsehood can be terribly destructive and should be resisted in proportion to the damage they are causing or threatening to cause. Here, too, God alone is perfect truth, incapable of deceiving or of being deceived, so what proceeds from the mouth of God is always true and need never be doubted. When His representatives speak His truth, or when they make a determination about something that is otherwise neutral, we should accept it without qualm or hesitation. But when they make a determination that appears contrary to some truth we already know by reason or by faith, then we have no choice but to refuse to accept it or abide by it.[12]

Obedience, then, is not given in a vacuum. While it is an obligation for an inferior (as such) to obey a superior (as such), this obligation relies on the presence of the foregoing conditions. On these points we may quote the plainspoken words of Archbishop Charles J. Chaput, O.F.M. Cap.:

> Christian obedience is never a form of unthinking servility. We have brains for a reason. Christian obedience is an act of love. It's a free gift of the self, and when obedience to authority becomes mechanical and excessive, or worse, if it serves a bad end, it crushes the spirit. All real love—and especially the love at the heart of a healthy obedience—is ordered to truth.... Life in the Church is no different. When authority undermines itself with corruption, falsehood, ambiguity, brutishness, cowardice, or mismanagement, fidelity to the truth requires faithful Christians to resist and challenge it.[13]

The hierarchy of authorities

What we must understand is that obedience is beautiful *because it is always obedience to GOD, whether immediately or mediately.* For example, when I worship God on the Lord's Day, I am doing so out of obedience to Him directly, because He is the one who has given the divine law that we must set aside one day of the week to worship Him. When I obey the pastors of the Church by assisting at Mass on Sunday, I am also obeying God, but indirectly, because the pastors who govern in His Name are the ones who established that particular determination of the precept. Similarly, when I obey legitimately-constituted civil authority, it is because it has its authority from God—not from the people. According to Pope Leo XIII, the one whom we must always obey—the only one whom we ultimately obey—is God Himself. It would be unworthy of human dignity, he says, that one man should have to submit to another man equal to him in nature, unless the ruler rules in God's name and by His authority, for then we are giving our assent to what God wills through His minister.[14]

The implications of this point are staggering. Immediately we understand why any human being, no matter what his position in the Church or in the State, is to be obeyed only if and when what he commands is in harmony with the law of God, or at very least not evidently opposed to it. If a civil law or an ecclesiastical law is at odds with the divine law or the natural law (which is the rational creature's participation in the eternal law of God's mind), then the principle memorably enunciated in the Acts of the Apostles takes force: "We must obey God rather than men." If one has a serious and well-founded *doubt* about whether the human command is compatible with the divine or natural law, one should not obey it. To say otherwise would be to say that in a case where we fear we might be committing a mortal sin, or even a venial sin, we should go ahead and do it lest we offend our superior.

Thus, obedience to anyone except to God is not an absolute and does not exist in a vacuum. It has conditions for its existence, levels at which it operates, and limits. A sound and sober analysis of this question is given by St. Thomas Aquinas in his *Summa theologiae*.[15] According to Aquinas, it belongs to the divine order that rulership is exercised not solely by God, whose will is always in accord with wisdom, but also by His representatives, whose will may not always be right: "It is written (Acts 5:29): *We ought to obey God rather than men*. Now sometimes the things commanded by a superior are against God. Therefore superiors are not to be obeyed in all things."[16] St. Thomas explains:

> There are two reasons for which a subject may not be bound to obey his superior in all things. First, on account of the command of a higher power. For

14

as a gloss says on Romans 13:2, "They that resist the power, resist the ordinance of God": "If a commissioner issue an order, are you to comply, if it is contrary to the bidding of the proconsul? Again if the proconsul command one thing, and the emperor another, will you hesitate to disregard the former and serve the latter? Therefore if the emperor commands one thing and God another, you must disregard the former and obey God" (cf. St. Augustine, *De Verb. Dom.* viii). Secondly, a subject is not bound to obey his superior if the latter command him to do something wherein he is not subject to him.[17]

To clarify further, the Angelic Doctor writes:

Man is subject to God simply as regards all things, both internal and external, wherefore he is bound to obey Him in *all* things. On the other hand, inferiors are not subject to their superiors in all things, but only in *certain* things and in a particular way, in respect of which the superior stands between God and his subjects, whereas in respect of other matters the subject is immediately under God, by Whom he is taught either by the natural or by the written law.[18]

Demands ...

Absolute obedience of creature

God:
Eternal Law

Absolute obedience of faith aided by reason

Revealed Divine Law
(includes liturgical providence)

Absolute obedience of reason aided by faith

Natural Law:
the rational creature's participation in eternal law

Conditional obedience based on trust, rightful subordination, preservation of ecclesiastical common good

Human Ecclesiastical Law:
Church Hierarchy / Religious Superiors
(given by a divinely established authority)

In order to be binding, this and each subsequent sphere of law must be in harmony with those above it.

Human Civil Law
(given by a divinely
established authority)

Conditional obedience based
on trust, rightful subordination,
preservation of civil common good

Family rules established by parents
(given by divinely established authority
through natural law; in various ways subject
to ecclesiastical and civil law)

Conditional obedience based
on trust, rightful subordination,
preservation of household
common good

Rules, policies, standards issued by voluntary associations
(e.g., private companies, clubs, unions): these are
not laws so much as agreed-upon conventions

Willing cooperation based on a
contract or implicit agreement

Accordingly, Aquinas distinguishes between three kinds of obedience: one that is "sufficient" for salvation, where one obeys what one must; another that is "perfect," whereby a religious vows himself to obey every lawful command given to him, no matter how onerous or displeasing; and finally, "indiscreet obedience," which "obeys even in matters unlawful."[19] Explaining why not every disobedience is a sin, he writes: "Although a man should take care to obey each superior, yet it is a greater duty to obey a higher than a lower authority, in sign of which the command of a lower authority is set aside if it be contrary to the command of a higher authority."[20] That great Thomist Leo XIII echoes his master when he says in his encyclical *Diuturnum Illud*:

> There is no reason why those who so behave themselves should be accused of refusing obedience; for, if the will of rulers is opposed to the will and the laws of God, they themselves exceed the bounds of their own power and pervert justice; nor can their authority then be valid, which, when there is no justice, is null. (n. 15)

In his encyclical *Libertas Praestantissimum* Leo XIII reinforces the point:

If, then, by anyone in authority, something be sanctioned out of conformity with the principles of right reason, and consequently hurtful to the commonwealth, such an enactment can have no binding force of law, as being no rule of justice, but certain to lead men away from that good which is the very end of civil society. (n. 10)

Though he says "civil society," the principle enunciated is true across the spectrum of all societies. Here we must do a bit of deeper digging to get at the root of authority itself, which Leo XIII correctly ties to the common good.[21]

The intrinsic relationship between authority and the common good

The good that relates people to one another is a *common* good, one that is good for many people at the same time without being diminished or divided.[22] Private goods get used up or removed from circulation when they are possessed. When a cake is divided up into pieces, each of us may get a piece (if we're lucky), but only I can eat mine and you yours. When I am wearing a piece of clothing, no one else can wear it simultaneously. Property, though it can be put to a hospitable and charitable use, is also limited in this way: by right and in practice, it is not equally everybody's to use, and it is diminished or worn out by use. A truly common good, on the other hand, can be shared simultaneously by many, perfecting them all. The peace of a family and the just ordering of a society are goods like this, since the more such a good exists, the more we all share in it, without its diminishment. Truth is a common good: if we both know the Pythagorean theorem, each of us possesses it completely and is perfected by it; now we can discuss it and make further discoveries from it. For these reasons, the common good is better than the private good—that is to say, it is better even for the individual than his merely individual good. This is important because it means that it will always be unreasonable to choose the merely individual good to the detriment of the common good. If the two come into conflict, the only reasonable thing to do is to choose the common good.[23]

Now, unlike the private good of individuals, who are already inclined by nature to seek their own good, the common good does not automatically take care of itself; it requires someone to care for it, act explicitly on its behalf, and coordinate individuals for its pursuit and its defense. This is the birth of authority: it is born to serve and promote the shared good of many. That is why authority can bind people to a certain course of action (or, conversely, forbid a course of action): the authority can, as it were, place the common good between the individual and his proposed course of action and say, in effect: "You can only do that by trampling the common good." That instantly makes the proposed course of action unreasonable, i.e., immoral. And if the authority says, "Do this," then it has placed the common good as an obstacle between the individual and *every other* course of action except the one commanded, so that *only* that one course of action is now reasonable.

Here is where we reach the heart of the question. An authority's power to morally bind resides in the common good, so if the authority deploys his office overtly *against* the common good, then that command inherently lacks moral binding power. He cannot say, "Unless you trample the common good, you will trample the common good." In other words, the goods that give rise to the power also limit it, such that the authority can act neither beyond nor against those goods. Obviously, this line of reasoning requires a distinction between "against the common good in a way where reasonable people could disagree" and "against the common good in a way where reasonable people could *not* disagree." The fact that we should disobey the President if he orders the military to destroy the United States does not mean that we can disobey him if he orders the military to engage in any war that we suspect will not turn out well.[24]

What, then, is the common good of the Church that accounts for her authority — an authority wielded to varying degrees by the individual members of the hierarchy and in a special way by the supreme pontiff? The Church's common good is the divine life of Jesus Christ, her sovereign Head — the superabundant grace of His divinized soul, shared with His members through the illumination of the intellect by revelation and the inflaming of the heart by the supernatural charity of His Heart — and the divinization of souls by the sacramental life and prayer (chiefly the solemn, formal, public worship we call the sacred liturgy). To this common good belongs the treasury of all the goods that God has revealed to us, all the goods Christ has obtained for us by His Most Precious Blood, and all the goods that the Father and the Son together have poured forth upon the Church by the descent of the Holy Spirit not only at the moment of Pentecost but, beginning then, over her entire history until the Second Coming.

Traditional liturgy as inherent to
the Church's common good

In the realm of the liturgy in particular, we must see the traditional rites of the Church as not merely human works but works conjointly of God and men — of the Church moved by the Holy Spirit.[25] Our Lord promised His disciples: "When He, the Spirit of Truth, is come, He will teach you all truth" (Jn 16:13). This promise includes the fullness of liturgy. One would expect, if the Church is truly governed by the Spirit of God, that her divine worship would, in its large lines and accepted forms, mature and become more perfect over time. As Dom Prosper Guéranger rhapsodizes:

It is in the holy Church that this divine Spirit dwells. He came down to her as an impetuous wind, and manifested Himself to her under the expressive symbol of tongues of fire. Ever since that day of Pentecost, He has dwelt in this His favoured bride. He is the principle of everything that is in her. He it is that prompts her prayers, her desires, her canticles of praise, her enthusiasm, and even her mourning. Hence her prayer is as uninterrupted as her existence. Day and night is her voice sounding sweetly in the ear of her divine Spouse, and her words are ever finding a welcome in His Heart....

Let not then the soul, the bride of Christ, that is possessed with a love of prayer, be afraid that her thirst cannot be quenched by these rich streams of the liturgy, which now flow calmly as a streamlet, now roll with the loud impetuosity of a torrent, and now swell with mighty heavings of the sea. Let her come and drink this clear water which springeth up unto life everlasting; for this water flows from the very fountains of her Saviour; and the Spirit of God animates it by His virtue, rendering it sweet and refreshing to the panting stag....

This renovative power of the liturgical year, to which we wish to draw the attention of our readers, is a mystery of the Holy Ghost, who unceasingly animates *the work which He has inspired the Church to establish among men*; that thus they might sanctify that time which has been given to them for the worship of their Creator.[26]

In a similar way (and practically at the same time), Guéranger's English contemporary John Henry Newman wrote:

When the last Apostle had been taken to his throne above, and the oracle of inspiration was for ever closed, when the faithful were left to that ordinary government which was intended to supersede the special season of miraculous action, then arose before their eyes in its normal shape and its full proportions that majestic Temple, of which the plans had been drawn out from the first by our Lord Himself amid His elect Disciples. Then was it that the Hierarchy came out in visible glory, and sat down on their ordained seats in the congregation of the faithful. Then followed in due course the holy periodical assemblies [the Councils], and the solemn rites of worship and the honour of sacred places, and the decoration of material structures; one appointment after another, realizing in act and deed the great idea which had been imparted to the Church since the day of Pentecost.[27]

If we take seriously this constructive and perfective role of the Holy Spirit across the Catholic centuries, we will understand why the rate of liturgical change *slows down* as liturgical rites, Eastern and Western, grow in their perfection until they have reached a certain maturity — a fullness of doctrinal expression, symbolic saturation, and artistic impressiveness — after which they cease to develop in any but incidental or minor ways. This fact — and it *is* a fact — explains the condemnation of false antiquarianism by Pope Pius XII, who noted that the earliest forms of ecclesial prayer are not to be deemed better or more authentic, since the Holy Spirit has always been at work in the ongoing enrichment and amplification of the liturgy.[28] As history demonstrates, the Spirit's work gradually shifts from inspiring altogether new prayers to preserving and hallowing the prayers already inspired, the worship already familiar, beloved, normative, and partaking in the qualities of God's revelation. It was and is no less a work of the Spirit to give Christians the grace of loving and maintaining their inheritance than it was to produce that inheritance in the first place. In the splendor of its monumental immutability, perfected ecclesial worship seems to come down to us not only from our ancestors but from the very court of heaven.

Speaking of the Mass in particular, the Bishop of Skopje, Macedonia, Smiljan Franjo Čekada, succinctly addressed his fellow conciliar fathers at the Second Vatican Council:

> The liturgy of the Mass, in which the Passion and Death of the Lord is re-presented for us, has acquired

its present form over the centuries. It has developed spontaneously and organically, gradually and successively—certainly under the influence of the Holy Spirit who is always present in the Church—from its primitive core to today's rite, full of harmony and beauty, capable of expressing in signs and words what it contains and signifies.[29]

In support of Bishop Čekada we can quote the magnificent words of the great Fr. Nicholas Gihr, writing at the end of the nineteenth century:

In the Eucharistic sacrifice the Catholic Church possesses the sun of her divine worship, the heart of her life of grace and virtue, her supreme good, her greatest wealth, and her most precious treasure. Hence she has ever exerted all her energy and care to celebrate this sublime and exalted mystery of faith in the most worthy manner. Christ Himself instituted and ordained merely the essential sacrificial act; but all that appertains to the liturgical development and investment of the divine sacrificial action, He left to His Church, directed and enlightened by the Holy Ghost. The sublime and inspiring sacrificial rite created by the Church is not a purely human production, but a work of art and a masterly achievement accomplished with the divine assistance: a sacred edifice so beautiful, so harmonious, so wonderful, so complete in its entirety as well as in its component parts, that the invisible hand of a heavenly wisdom, which directed the erection and execution of it, cannot be mistaken and should not be heedlessly overlooked.[30]

About the Roman Canon in particular, Fr. Gihr writes:

The Canon is, through its origin, antiquity, and use, venerable and inviolable and sacred. If ever a prayer of the Church came into existence under the special inspiration of the Holy Ghost, it is assuredly the prayer of the Canon.[31]

Now, because all this is true — it is the only way Catholics ever thought about their liturgy prior to about the middle of the twentieth century — it follows that the traditional liturgical worship of the Church, her *lex orandi* or law of prayer, is a fundamental, normative, and immutable expression of her *lex credendi* or law of belief, one that cannot be contradicted or abolished or heavily rewritten without rejecting the Spirit-led continuity of the Catholic

Church as a whole.[32] Massimo Viglione elucidates this point:

> The *lex orandi* of the Church, in fact, is not a "precept" of positive law voted on by a parliament or prescribed by a sovereign, which can always be retracted, changed, replaced, improved, or worsened. The *lex orandi* of the Church, furthermore, is not a specific and determined "thing" in time and space, as much as it is the collective whole of theological and spiritual norms and liturgical and pastoral practices of the entire history of the Church, from evangelical times—and specifically from Pentecost—up to today. Although it obviously lives in the present, it is rooted in the entire past of the Church. Therefore, we are not talking here about something human—exclusively human—that the latest boss can change at his pleasure. The *lex orandi* comprises all twenty centuries of the history of the Church, and there is no man or group of men in the world who can change this twenty-century-old deposit. There is no pope, council, or episcopate that can change the Gospel, the *Depositum Fidei*, or the universal Magisterium

of the Church. Nor can the Liturgy of all time be [decisively] changed.[33]

Dismissing the notion that attachment to the old rite is a matter of sentimentality or aesthetics, Bishop Vitus Huonder focuses squarely on its confessional content:

The rite as we have it is a profession of faith, and a profession of faith cannot be simply set aside. What can you say if, as a bishop, I stopped praying the Apostles' Creed? What would these faithful say about me? They would say to me: "What's the matter with you, that is not possible!" We must not forget that the traditional [Roman] rite, especially because it has the weight of years, this maturity, is also a profession of faith. They cannot demand that the faithful put aside this profession of faith.[34]

As Church history attests, the Mass has been repeatedly proved to be just such a profession of faith, above all by the actions of those seeking to undermine that faith. The *Catholic Encyclopedia* is quite clear on this point:

That the Mass … is the central feature of the Catholic religion hardly needs to be said. During the Reformation and always, the Mass has been the test. The word of the Reformers: "It is the Mass that matters," was true. The Cornish insurgents in 1549 rose against the new religion, and expressed their whole cause in their demand to have the Prayer-book Communion Service taken away and the old Mass restored. The long persecution of Catholics in England took the practical form of laws chiefly against saying Mass; for centuries the occupant of the English throne was obliged to manifest his Protestantism, not by a general denial of the whole system of Catholic dogma but by a formal repudiation of the doctrine of Transubstantiation and of the Mass. As union with Rome is the bond between Catholics, so is our common share in this, the most venerable rite in Christendom, the witness and safeguard of that bond.[35]

For precisely this reason, only two groups of Catholics (or, I should say, former Catholics) ever questioned the traditional *lex orandi*: the Protestants, who rejected it because they openly dissented from the *lex credendi* it expressed, and the Modernists, who believed that the *lex credendi* perpetually evolves and must evolve, and therefore the *lex orandi* must be mutable and malleable to keep up with it. We can be more specific: both Protestants and Modernists regard the post-Constantinian history of the Catholic Church as one of progressive darkening and pagan relapsation, a deviation from the pure, simple, authentic springtime of the early Christians who met in homes to "break bread" and remember Jesus, the wonder-working carpenter from Nazareth. According to this view, the deviation reached its nadir in the Middle Ages, which then transmitted a superstitious cult to succeeding centuries, culminating in the courtly clericalist dumb-show known as the Tridentine Mass. The fiery breath of the Pentecostal spirit melted this paradigm and replaced it with forms of worship more in tune with the living faith of Christians: first in the Reformation, then, much later, in the period of Vatican II and the sweeping reforms it ushered in.

> The traditional liturgical worship of the Church, her *lex orandi* or law of prayer, is a fundamental, normative, and immutable expression of her *lex credendi* or law of belief.

There is practically no mainstream book on liturgy from about 1965 to about 2005 that does not express something like this viewpoint, with varying degrees of mockery for the past and varying degrees of confidence for a glorious future of vernacular, accessible, lay-inclusive worship. It simply was the unquestioned self-critique of the Church by her self-styled experts. It is no exaggeration to say that the liturgical reform under Paul VI rested on a Protestant understanding of Church history and liturgy. To accept it is to accept, to a greater or lesser extent, a vision of Catholicism as a history of obscurantism, mystification, ritualistic clericalism, and systematic exclusion of believers from the liberties of the Gospel—in a word, a history of corruption that could never be the fruit of the Holy Spirit. Those who support traditional worship are therefore also obscurantists, mystifiers, ritualists, clericalists, and elite pharisees who are guilty of opposing the Holy Spirit.[36]

The pope who sets himself against the common good

And I'm afraid this is *exactly* the point of view that stands behind the motu proprio *Traditionis Custodes* and all who support it. It is a profoundly uncatholic, indeed anti-Catholic, point of view. Since the liturgy truly is the "font and apex of the Christian life," the home of divine revelation and the primary agent of our transformation in Christ, it follows that to abolish or prohibit or in any way work against the venerable Roman Rite that was humbly received, gratefully loved, and lavishly praised for century after century of uninterrupted growth is the most notorious and damaging attack on the common good possible or imaginable. If *this* is not the kind of good the Church's authority exists to protect, one may well ask what goods would qualify? As a statement from the Society of St. Pius X correctly argues:

> The traditional Mass belongs to the most intimate part of the common good in the Church. Restricting it, pushing it into ghettos, and ultimately planning its demise, can have no legitimacy. This law is not a law of the Church, because, as St. Thomas says, a law against the common good is no valid law.[37]

Catholic tradition recognizes the pope's solemn duty toward the immemorial liturgical practice of the Church.[38] According to the famous Papal Oath of the *Liber Diurnus Romanorum Pontificum*, a handbook of formularies used by the pontifical chancellery at the end of the first millennium, the pope is to swear: "I shall keep inviolate the discipline and ritual of the Church just as I found and received it handed down by my predecessors."[39] In one of its approved texts, the Council of Constance states: "Since the Roman Pontiff exercises such great power among mortals, it is right that he be bound all the more by the incontrovertible bonds of the faith and by the rites that are to be observed regarding the Church's Sacraments."

Of very many theological authorities who might be brought forward, let it suffice to summon Francisco Suárez, S.J. (1548–1617):

> If the Pope lays down an order contrary to right customs, one does not have to obey him; if he tries to do something manifestly opposed to justice and to the common good, it would be licit to resist him; if he attacks by force, he could be repelled by force, with the moderation characteristic of a good defense.[40]

Suárez moreover claims that the pope could be schismatic "if he wanted to overturn all the ecclesiastical ceremonies resting on apostolic tradition."[41] The idea seems to be that it is always legitimate for us to wish to adhere to that which the Church has solemnly taught *and practiced*. Already in the fourth century, St. Athanasius the Great could say to the faithful: "For our canons *and our forms* were not given to the Churches at the present day, but were wisely and safely transmitted to us from our forefathers."[42] We ought to be skeptical of novelties that certain churchmen wish to add to the tradition or substitute for it and should be prepared to offer resistance if an attempt is made to eliminate tradition, which is unquestionably an essential and constitutive part of the Church's common good.[43] As the fictional bishop Edmund Forster says in Fr. Bryan Houghton's classic work *Mitre & Crook*: "Fancy having to defend the [Tridentine] Mass by legal quibbles. What nonsense! It stands *mole sua*, by its own imponderable weight. It is the Mass."[44] Martin Mosebach makes the same point:

> Pope Benedict did not "allow" the "old Mass," and he granted no privilege to celebrate it. In a word, he did not take a disciplinary measure that a successor can retract. What was new and surprising about *Summorum Pontificum* was that it declares that the celebration of the old Mass does not need any permission. It had never been forbidden because it never could be forbidden. One could conclude that here we find a fixed, insuperable limit to the authority of a pope. Tradition stands above the pope. The old Mass, rooted deep in the first Christian millennium, is as a matter of principle beyond the pope's authority to prohibit.[45]

In his gentle way, Cardinal Sarah voices the same opinion in his commentary on the famous words of Benedict XVI:

> What is sacred for the Church, then, is the unbroken chain that links her with certainty to Jesus. A chain of faith without rupture or contradiction, a chain of prayer and liturgy without breakage or disavowal. Without this radical continuity, what credibility could the Church still claim? In her, there is no turning back, but an organic and continuous development that we call the living tradition. The sacred cannot be decreed, it is received from God and passed on.
>
> This is undoubtedly the reason for which Benedict XVI could authoritatively affirm: "In the history of the liturgy there is growth and progress, but no rupture. What earlier generations held as sacred, remains sacred and great for us too, and it cannot be all of a sudden entirely forbidden or even considered harmful. It behooves all of us to preserve the riches which have developed in the Church's faith and prayer, and to give them their proper place."[46]

Francis's contradiction of his predecessor on this point is obvious, for *Traditionis Custodes*'s fundamental message is: "What earlier generations held as sacred does *not* remain sacred and great for us too, and it *can* be all of a sudden entirely forbidden and considered harmful. It does *not* behoove all of us to preserve the riches which have developed in the Church's faith and prayer, or to give them any place at all."[47] José Antonio Ureta explains that our refusal to comply with Pope Francis's motu proprio "is not a matter of questioning papal authority, before which our love and reverence must grow. It is love for the papacy itself that must lead to the denunciation of *Traditionis Custodes*, which seeks dictatorially to eliminate the most ancient and venerable rite of Catholic worship, from which all the faithful have the right to drink."[48]

Notice that Suárez speaks of "all the ecclesiastical ceremonies resting on apostolic tradition," *apostolica traditione firmatas*: he's talking about the whole structure that has been raised upon apostolic origins. That would mean something like the 1570 *Missale Romanum*, which St. Pius V defined as a "pure liturgy ... in accord with the rites and customs of the Roman Church," and which he exalted as an ensign above the chaos of the Reformation.[49] Contrary to the superficial line taken by some Catholic apologists today, St. Pius V's Apostolic Constitution *Quo Primum* is not "just a disciplinary document" that can be readily set aside or contradicted by his successors. Since the liturgy itself concerns matters of faith and morals, *Quo Primum* must be considered a document *de rebus fidei et morum*, and therefore its substantive content is not susceptible to being set aside by a later pontiff—a status acknowledged by the eloquent gesture of those of his successors who, when promulgating new editions of the Roman Missal, were careful always to preface them with *Quo Primum*, showing that they accepted and embraced that which Pius V had codified and canonized.[50] The pope didn't cause the Mass to become inviolable by publishing *Quo Primum*, but rather, *Quo Primum* was inviolable because of the Mass. This Apostolic Constitution could only have been promulgated, and can only be coherently understood, as the proper maintenance of an extant, already-inviolable traditional Mass. Hence, *Quo Primum*'s witness to the perennial *lex orandi* and *lex credendi* of the Church of Rome remains in force, guaranteeing the perpetual rights of the Tridentine Mass as well as of the Latin-rite clergy to celebrate it:

> In virtue of Our Apostolic authority, We grant and concede in perpetuity that, for the chanting or reading of the Mass in any church whatsoever, this Missal is hereafter to be followed absolutely, without any scruple of conscience or fear of incurring any penalty, judgment, or censure, and may freely and lawfully be used.

Nor are superiors, administrators, canons, chaplains, and other secular priests, or religious, of whatever title designated, obliged to celebrate the Mass otherwise than as enjoined by Us. We likewise declare and ordain ... that this present document cannot be revoked or modified, but remains always valid and retains its full force.... Would anyone, however, presume to commit such an act [i.e., altering *Quo Primum*], he should know that he will incur the wrath of Almighty God and of the Blessed Apostles Peter and Paul.[51]

Now I am aware that there are intricate questions around *Quo Primum*. It does have disciplinary aspects to it, so it's not simply a declaration concerning matters of faith and morals; yet it is also not simply an administrative decree that can be overturned or cancelled entirely: it has far more weight than that. *Quo Primum* defines the missal of 1570 as the monument of tradition par excellence for the Roman Rite, the authoritative expression of the *lex orandi* of the Roman Church. It is the Mass of the Western Fathers. As such, it can never be rendered illegitimate in the Catholic Church, or in need of a massive overhaul. If Pius V was simply "modifying the Missal for the needs of his time" (as has been inanely alleged), why would he dream of giving a permanent sanction for the use of his

Missal, calling down the wrath of the Apostles on those who would act against it? He obviously believed this was the core of the Roman liturgical tradition, which no earthly power could undo.[52]

It is love for the papacy itself that must lead to the denunciation of *Traditionis Custodes*, which seeks dictatorially to eliminate the most ancient and venerable rite of Catholic worship.

We may tie all of the preceding points together in a syllogism. The Tridentine Profession of Faith recognizes, as essential to Catholicity, adherence to "received and approved ceremonies of the Catholic Church in the solemn administration of all the sacraments" (i.e., the traditional rites).[53] *Quo Primum* recognizes the *Missale Romanum* of 1570 as the traditional rite of the Mass—*that*, and not a mere positive law, is the basis of its perpetual standing. Therefore, adherence to the liturgy codified and canonized in this *Missale Romanum* is essential to Catholicity in the sphere of the Latin-rite Church: it is what makes one a Roman Catholic. A corollary follows: the rejection of traditional rites as an authoritative criterion, and the embrace of a non-traditional missal, makes one ... something else!

I am assuming that the reader already understands that the classical Roman Rite and the modern rite of Paul VI are *two different liturgical rites*—so different in their content, which includes texts, music, rubrics, ceremonies, and appurtenances, that the latter cannot by any stretch of the imagination be seen as merely a "revision" or "new version" of the former.[54] Pope Paul VI implicitly recognized the rupture by being the first pope in four hundred years to omit Pius V's bull *Quo Primum* and to replace it with a constitution sardonically named *Missale Romanum*. As if drawing out the meaning of Montini's gesture, Pope Francis has stated twice, subsequent to *Traditionis Custodes*, that the current situation in the Church of Rome is akin to *biritualism* (although it would perhaps be more accurate to use the word "bipolarity").[55] This point is important: we are not dealing with just another slightly revised version of the same missal, but a true rupture such that there are *two* "Roman Rites" with conflicting and competing causes, principles, elements, and manifestations—an unprecedented and incomprehensible situation, and the root of all of our present liturgical troubles.[56]

The *sensus fidelium* and the resistance of a Catholic conscience

I mentioned earlier that we do not owe obedience to an ecclesiastical authority if he acts against the common good of the Church. It is important to note that Catholic theologians are unanimous in maintaining that this is possible—such an authority can actually *act against the common good*—and, even more importantly, that ordinary Catholics are capable of recognizing *when* it is happening. If we could not, we would be helpless to respond to any moral or intellectual deviations on the part of our pastors and teachers. For that matter, if the faithful lacked this capacity of discernment, much of Church history would be unintelligible. Take the staunch and public refusal of many Catholics in England to attend Archbishop Cranmer's new, protestantized rite of Mass,[57] even when they were encouraged to do so by clergy who preferred the strategy of compromise with the heretical forces coming to power there in the sixteenth century. Even at the cost of inconvenience, harassment, fines, and worse penalties, devout English Catholics refused to attend what would only later be called the *Anglican* rite—and this, well before any directive from Rome asserted that the new service was "the offspring of schism, the badge of hatred of the Church," and "grievously sinful" to attend.[58]

A valuable exposition of the traditional view of the *sensus fidelium*—the capacity, enjoyed by the baptized members of the Church, to discern the truth of Christ if they have been formed properly by it and are striving to live according to it—may be found in a 2014 document prepared by the International Theological Commission of the Vatican. Although not magisterial, this document accurately conveys the consensus of the theologians of all times:

> "Beloved, do not believe every spirit, but test the spirits to see whether they are from God; for many false prophets have gone out into the world" (1 Jn 4:1). The *sensus fidei fidelis* confers on the believer the capacity to discern whether or not a teaching or practice is coherent with the true faith by which he or she already lives.... The *sensus fidei fidelis* also enables individual believers to perceive any disharmony, incoherence, or contradiction between a teaching or practice and the authentic Christian faith by which they live. They react as a music lover does to false notes in the performance of a piece of music. In such cases, believers interiorly resist the teachings or practices concerned and do not accept them or participate in them. [As St. Thomas says:]

"The *habitus* of faith possesses a capacity whereby, thanks to it, the believer is prevented from giving assent to what is contrary to the faith, just as chastity gives protection with regard to whatever is contrary to chastity."[59]

Remarkably for our day and age, the ITC document goes on to say:

Alerted by their *sensus fidei*, individual believers may deny assent even to the teaching of legitimate pastors if they do not recognise in that teaching the voice of Christ, the Good Shepherd. "The sheep follow [the Good Shepherd] because they know his voice. They will not follow a stranger, but they will run away from him because they do not know the voice of strangers" (Jn 10:4–5). For St. Thomas, a believer, even without theological competence, can and even must resist, by virtue of the *sensus fidei*, his or her bishop if the latter preaches heterodoxy. In such a case, the believer does not treat himself or herself as the ultimate criterion of the truth of faith, but rather, faced with materially "authorized" preaching which he or she finds troubling, without being able to explain exactly why, defers assent and appeals interiorly to the superior authority of the universal Church.[60]

What is this Spirit-guided infallibility of the *sensus fidelium*? It is just the super-charged version of the reality that we cannot abdicate our personal reason or our "Christian common sense." Even as secular rulers do not have an authority that simply overrides a citizen's own exercise of reason and the voice of his conscience, so too in the realm of grace ecclesiastical rulers do not have an authority that simply shuts down the believer's reason and evacuates his responsibility before God to love the Church's common good more than any personal good of anyone.[61] The *sensus fidelium* is part and parcel of the Church's indefectibility, which is too often falsely construed as a kind of top-down, hierarchy-only, magisterial quality, when in point of fact it is a divine endowment made to the Church precisely as a *corporate entity*. That is why Newman could observe that during the Arian crisis of the fourth century, "the divine dogma of Our Lord's divinity was proclaimed, enforced, maintained, and (humanly speaking) preserved, far more by the 'Ecclesia docta' [the taught Church] than by the 'Ecclesia docens' [the teaching Church]" and that "the body of the episcopate was unfaithful to its commission, while the body of the laity was faithful to its baptism."[62]

The mention of conscience necessitates a brief digression on this much-abused word, which nevertheless names a reality of great importance.

> We do not owe obedience to an ecclesiastical authority if he acts against the common good of the Church.

In the sixties, seventies, and eighties, making a big deal of "conscience" was the province of progressives trying to dissent from perennial teaching such as the ban on contraception (which Paul VI confirmed but by no means invented). Liberals continue to deploy the word as a cover for immoral acts, especially against the sixth and ninth commandments. For them, "conscience" seems to mean something like "my desires as an autonomous modern person uninformed by or unwilling to submit to God's law." This politicized distortion gave rise to an opposite reaction among conservatives and traditionalists, who likewise abused the word by making a "well-formed conscience" equivalent to "automatic submission to external authority," which, in keeping with neo-ultramontanism, came down to the will of the pope as the one and only principle of action necessary for virtuous Catholics.[63] The result of this tug-of-war between factions within the Church is that the concept of conscience has all but lost its meaning; it has been evacuated of its substantive content. We have all—liberals, conservatives, and traditionalists alike—let slip our hold on an element of what makes us distinctively human, that is, rational, free, responsible beings before God.

According to St. Thomas, "conscience is...an activity, namely, the actual application of moral knowledge to conduct" in the here and now.[64] St. John Henry Newman characterized conscience as "a messenger of Him, who, both in nature and in grace, speaks to us behind a veil, and teaches and rules us by His representatives."[65] The Second Vatican Council rightly praised this messenger: "Deep within his conscience man discovers a law which he has not laid upon himself but which he must obey. Its voice, ever calling him to love and to do what is good and to avoid evil, sounds in his heart at the right moment.... For man has in his heart a law inscribed by God."[66] To hear this voice, one must "turn inward," says St. Augustine, "and in everything you do, see God as your witness."[67] In these statements we see a link between conscience as an inner law or voice, and an external standard or authority that it heeds. According to the *Catechism of* the Catholic Church, moral conscience "bears witness to the authority of truth in reference to the supreme Good to which the human person is drawn, and it welcomes the commandments."[68] Conscience is always linked to true doctrine, a source of illumination that imposes itself upon the receptive mind as the truth. As long as conscience is sensitive to its own neediness, it seeks a trustworthy light for its own formation and is only at rest, illuminated, when and as long as it has found one. Commenting on the verse "the water that I will give him, shall become in him a fountain" (Jn 4:14), St. Thomas writes: "one who drinks by believing in Christ draws in a fountain of water; and when he draws it in, his conscience, which is the heart of the inner man, begins to live and it itself becomes a fountain."[69]

Conscience, therefore, certainly does not mean "what I feel like doing or not doing." It points to the activity in the human soul of judging what is right or wrong, in conformity with the known truth, so that we may in turn *will* what is right to be done at this moment, in this situation. Conscience works hand in hand with the virtue of prudence, by which we discern the best course of action given all the pertinent circumstances as well as the inherent requirements of virtue, which always bind us to the law of God, for our own good.

Psalm 118[119], the longest psalm in the Psalter of David and a backbone of the Divine Office, emphatically repeats that God's law is our guide, our illumination, our freedom, our delight, and that we will not be able to judge rightly apart from it. Continual meditation on God's law, as given to us in Scripture and Tradition, is the divinely bestowed means by which our power of moral judgment is to be shaped.

If we understand, then, how both conscience and virtue operate, we will see that there can be no such thing as "blind obedience" in the Christian life. To do anything good and to avoid evil, we must make a judgment about the good to be done or the evil to be avoided; we must engage in practical reasoning about any proposed course of action; we must interiorly will conformity to the truth and reject falsehood. While there are general rules of action and exceptionless norms, only the individual can, at the moment of acting, know and choose what is right to do or not do; this responsibility over oneself cannot be "outsourced" to someone else who will think and choose for him.[70] Of course, there will be times when a command is given to someone who is under another's authority and the subordinate sees no moral difficulty in it; in that situation, the lack of anything objectionable in the command would free him to follow it without further ado. The point here is not that moral reasoning must be complicated and time-consuming—a virtuous person with an illuminated conscience will find certain decisions very easy to make, even if the consequence will be suffering—but rather, that moral reasoning is *always* going on and cannot be circumvented, nor should any attempt be made to do so in the name of a purportedly "holier" form of obedience. Although the ecclesiastical Magisterium furnishes principles by which we can discern virtuous actions and can know that we must refrain from certain kinds of actions that are intrinsically evil, only an individual Christian can posit the *moral action* that consists in following and applying principles in his personal decisions; no external source can step in and take over this function of his soul, for which he will be accountable before God. This, rightly understood, is the primacy of conscience to which the Catholic tradition bears witness.[71]

Today, a true appeal to conscience can and should be made by Catholics who see vital goods being violently taken from them or evils being pressed on them. This is not to be "progressive"; it is to be *human* and *Christian*. It is to be rightly traditional, knowing and witnessing to the perennial value of what has been loved and venerated before us and was always handed down with unwavering fidelity.

We are not the revolutionaries or the disobedient

Let us be absolutely clear about this: to attack the traditional Latin Mass (or any of the traditional liturgical rites) is to attack the Providence of God the Father; to reject the work of Christ, the King and Lord of history; to blaspheme the fruitfulness of the Holy Ghost in the Church's life of prayer. It is contrary to the practice of every age of the Church, of every saint, council, and pope prior to the twentieth century. It contradicts several key virtues of the Christian life, most notably religion, gratitude, and humility. It implies the rejection of the dogmatic confession of faith contained in the traditional Latin *lex orandi* in its organic unfolding over at least 1,600 years, which is contrary to the theological virtue of faith; it implies the rejection of the communion of the saints in a common lineage and patrimony of ecclesiastical worship, which is contrary to the theological virtue of charity. In all these ways and more, the postconciliar liturgical reform, its subsequent ruthless implementation, and Pope Francis's renewed efforts to extinguish the preceding tradition are unreasonable, unjust, and unholy, and therefore cannot be accepted as legitimate or embraced as the will of God.[72] As St. Thomas Aquinas famously says: unjust laws "are acts of violence rather than laws ... Wherefore they do not bind in conscience."[73] A repudiation of our Catholic liturgical patrimony is tantamount to disobedience to God; and we will be obedient to God through our "disobedience" to the revolutionaries. In the words of eminent Church historian Roberto de Mattei:

> Against the philosophy of revolt, against the philosophy of dissent, against the philosophy of the Revolution, which has the devil as its prime inspiration, we oppose with the philosophy of obedience to the Divine Law, violated and offended all over the world. It is for the sake of this supreme obedience that we are ready to withdraw our obedience to men, even those of the Church, if grave circumstances require it. But if this happens, we do so with sorrow, we do so with respect, by renewing our spirit of obedience to God and His Law, renewing our love for the Church and our neighbor: to every brother, whose will we wish to do, according to the priorities of dependency and hierarchy which regulate the universe. We love order and we combat disorder. Our struggle against disorder is called Counter-Revolution, a movement whereby order is re-established and restored.[74]

Along the same lines Sebastian Morello writes:

Those Catholics who are anxiously conserving their inherited religious beliefs and practices are not the revolutionaries, and they are not the disobedient. Shamefully, such Catholics will be accused — indeed, already are being accused — of disobedience. In reality, such Catholics simply do not want to be part of a revolutionary cause. It is precisely their obedience and fidelity to their tradition, in the face of the abusive exercise of arbitrary power, that makes them the targets of revolution and disobedience. Such Catholics must be clear about this in their minds: they are not the revolutionaries; they are not the disobedient; they are the faithful.[75]

If we are convinced that something essential, something decisive in the Faith is under attack from the pope or any other hierarch, we are not only permitted to refuse to do what is being asked or commanded, not only permitted to refuse to give up what is being unjustly taken away or forbidden; we are *obliged* to refuse, out of the love we bear to Our Lord Himself, our love for His Mystical Body, and our proper love for our own souls. Sitting on the fence is not an option: as a good priest put it, "the fence has been electrified."[76] Our obedience is rightfully given to the higher authority: in the matter under discussion, that means to Divine Providence, to the Holy Spirit, to the authority of the Church of all ages, to the voice of God in one's conscience as it bears witness to the greater sacrality and sanctifying power of the ancient rites and to the needs and demands of the ecclesial common good.[77]

> A repudiation of our Catholic
> liturgical patrimony is tantamount
> to disobedience to God; and we will
> be obedient to God through our
> "disobedience" to the revolutionaries.

Because this is true, any penalty or punishment meted out for "disobedience" to the revolutionaries would be *illicit.* If a punishment is given on false theological or canonical premises, it is null and void, just as the canonical trial and excommunication of Joan of Arc were recognized as illegitimate twenty-five years after her execution at the hands of corrupt and politically-motivated clergy. Imagine a hierarch who removes, suspends, excommunicates, or seeks to laicize a Catholic priest because the priest loves and adheres to the liturgical tradition and the hierarch despises and rejects it.[78] The suspension or excommunication or even removal from the clerical state would be null and void: it is a self-contradiction for authority to be used against anyone whose only "crime" is that he "contends earnestly for the faith once delivered to the saints" (cf. Jude 3). The priest may continue administering the sacraments as before; his faculties remain unimpaired.[79]

Someone might object that I am, in essence, denying that legitimate ecclesiastical authority still exists, for if it did, any penalty it meted out against a priest, whether guilty or innocent, would still be effective *pro tempore*: a priest who had his faculties removed would lack faculties. After all, canon law assumes the validity of actions in the external forum. My response is that this reasoning would be true in ordinary times but not in our extraordinary times, when ecclesiastical authority, by its assault on liturgical and theological tradition, has turned against the common good of the Church, subverting its own purpose and, to that extent, its authority. Catholics recognize a law more fundamental than canonical dictates, one that conditions them necessarily and thoroughly: *salus animarum suprema lex*, the salvation of souls is the supreme law. It is for the salvation of souls that the entire structure of ecclesiastical law exists; it has no other purpose than ultimately to protect and advance the sharing of the life of Christ with mankind.

In normal circumstances, ecclesiastical laws create a structure within which the Church's mission may unfold in an orderly and peaceful way. But there can be situations of anarchy or breakdown, corruption or apostasy, where the ordinary structures become *impediments* to, not facilitators of, the Church's mission. In these cases, the voice of conscience dictates that one should do what needs to be done, in prudence and charity, for the achievement of the sovereign law. For example, St. Athanasius the Great was officially excommunicated but did not hesitate to carry on with his work nonetheless,[80] and many priests who remained faithful amid the extinction of the Catholic hierarchy in Elizabethan England exercised their ministry in violation of ordinary canonical norms, even over multiple generations. When a building is burning down, one tries to put out the fire and rescue victims with any means at hand, rather than waiting until the fire brigade arrives—especially if one knows from bitter experience that the fire chief is absent from his post, or sleeping, or intoxicated, or convinced that fires are beneficial, and most of the firemen are bumblers whose methods don't work, or, worse, are paid by saboteurs to spray gasoline on the fire. The crisis in the Church is not to be blamed on those who, conscious of an obligation in the sight of God and a duty to suffering fellow believers, have responded to it as best they can, with the bright weapons of obedience to the highest law that governs all others. I can only echo the sentiments of Archbishop Viganò:

> Let us not make the mistake of presenting the current events as "normal," judging what happens with the legal, canonical, and sociological parameters that such normality would presuppose. In extraordinary times — and the present crisis in the Church is indeed extraordinary — events go beyond the ordinary known to our fathers. In extraordinary times, we can hear a pope deceive the faithful; see Princes of the Church accused of crimes that in other times would have aroused horror and been met with severe punishment; witness in our churches liturgical rites that seem to have been invented by Cranmer's perverse mind; see prelates process the unclean idol of the Pachamama into St. Peter's Basilica; and hear the Vicar of Christ apologize to the worshippers of that *simulacrum* if a Catholic dares to throw it into the Tiber.[81]

As His Excellency has frequently reminded us, the situation in the Church is paralleled by, and intertwined with, the crisis unfolding simultaneously in the secular political realm. The abuse of authority, the scare tactics, the attempted punishments, and the courageous response called for are analogous:

At this point, citizens on the one hand and the faithful on the other find themselves in the condition of having to disobey earthly authority in order to obey divine authority, which governs nations and the Church. Obviously the "reactionaries"—that is, those who do not accept the perversion of authority and want to remain faithful to the Church of Christ and to their homeland—constitute an element of dissent that cannot be tolerated in any way, and therefore they must be discredited, delegitimized, threatened and deprived of their rights in the name of a "public good" that is no longer the *bonum commune* but its contrary. Whether accused of conspiracy theories, traditionalism, or fundamentalism, these few survivors of a world that they want to make disappear constitute a threat to the accomplishment of the global plan, just at the most crucial moment of its realization.... We can therefore understand the violence of the reactions of authority and prepare ourselves for a strong and determined opposition, continuing to avail ourselves of those rights that have been abusively and illicitly denied us.[82]

It is for the salvation of souls that the entire structure of ecclesiastical law exists.

Stand firm and hold fast

Traditionis Custodes has, ironically, vindicated the basic traditionalist claim that a rupture has occurred between the Church of the ages and the conciliar Church, or at very least, between the worship offered by the one and that offered by the other. In that case, however, the "loser" is not the Church of the ages, with her fixed dogmas and her grand liturgy; the loser would have to be the latecomer, the parvenu, the imposter. That is why it is a *necessity*, not a luxury, for some priests and religious in the Church to bear witness by their very lives—by their consistent, principled, integral fidelity to tradition—that the Church must be indefectibly the same as she ever was, and that what was sacred and great in the past can never fail to be so in the present and until the end of time. The moment tradition is proscribed, so is the Church's substantive continuity, and with it, the basis of ecclesiastical authority, since the episcopacy and the papacy are themselves transmitted to us by tradition.[83] As George Neumayr witheringly observes:

> For a religion predicated on tradition, the suppression of tradition makes no sense unless the goal is to change that religion fundamentally.... The pope, of course, embodies the very division that he claims to deplore. He is dividing Catholics at the deepest possible level—from Catholic tradition itself. A "unity" rooted in heterodoxy is a sham.... By disregarding the authority of past popes, Francis erases his own.[84]

Today, the ecclesial witness of the ancient, medieval, and Tridentine heritage is gravely endangered, not only by the actions of hierarchs who wish to sever themselves from Tradition but also by the aggressive overreach of civic leaders intent on making divine worship subservient to the rising cult of "population health." It must be clearly understood that no officeholder in either the Church or the State has authority in natural, divine, or ecclesiastical law to prohibit Mass or refuse the Sacraments to otherwise well-disposed Catholic faithful.[85] The *salus animarum* can never be replaced with the *sanitas corporis* as the supreme law of the Church—as if a clean bill of health, polyester facemask, or vaccine passport could ever be required as a necessary precondition for attending the Sacrifice of Calvary. In the convicting words of Bishop Athanasius Schneider, many Catholic clergy have "lost a supernatural vision and have abandoned the primacy of the eternal good of souls."[86] Cancellations of Mass in the name of community health concerns have shown that we are in earnest need of reclaiming that supernatural vision, if a truly fitting worship of God is to continue in our sanctuaries.[87]

The most valuable contribution in our age of amnesia and confusion will therefore be made by those who do not content themselves with admiring from a distance or occasionally lending a hand to the restoration and defense of our sacred heritage, but who personally *identify with* the enduring truth and goodness of that heritage by taking it on as the mode in which they will live their daily lives. The clergy who are committed exclusively to the old rite as a matter of principle must not compromise, regardless of threats or penalties. Rather, they should understand the legal emptiness of these baseless maneuvers to stifle it. Now that our enemies have made it clear that they intend our eventual liquidation, classic legal principles of self-defense, proportionate resistance, and the invalidity of unjustly imposed penalties come fully into play.

No officeholder in either the Church or
the State has authority in natural, divine,
or ecclesiastical law to prohibit Mass
or refuse the Sacraments to otherwise
well-disposed Catholic faithful.

Some priests may succeed in evading or flouting unjust laws (whether issued by ecclesiastical or civil authorities) for years or decades, but others will be turned in by pursuivants or otherwise called on the carpet. Their superiors may declare their faculties removed or order them to relocate; they may be suspended and deprived of wages; they might even be excommunicated, although that is unlikely. What they should bear in mind, however, is that as long as the sole reason for disciplinary action is their principled adherence to the traditional rites of the Roman Church, such penalties will be null and void, and their priestly ministry may continue unabated.[88] Under a different pope or a different bishop, saner policies will prevail and accounts can then be set to rights, the irregular paperwork rectified.[89] Precisely because, in Cardinal Müller's words, "the good shepherd can be recognized by the fact that he worries more about the salvation of souls than about recommending himself to a higher authority by subservient 'good behavior,'"[90] courageous pastors and canceled priests will find themselves promptly and generously supported by grateful laity who will rally behind them to defend their sanctuaries, provide for their material needs, and, if worse comes to worst, furnish a dignified place for Mass to be offered. As I recalled elsewhere:

> Traditional Catholic worship and the way of life it sustains was saved in the late sixties and seventies by priests and laity willing to do exactly this, and nothing less, to remain true to what they knew to be true. It was initially a tiny minority who kept the flame burning and who spread it, one person at a time, across the world. Very often they had to do so outside of the official structures of the Church, or rather, outside of the self-endorsing legal fictions of churchmen and their self-destructive "renewal." They were, for a time, "pastors out in the cold," but they would never exchange their clean conscience, Catholic integrity, pastoral fruitfulness, and spiritual consolation for any emoluments from a corrupt and corrosive system.[91]

The traditional priest may continue with a serene conscience, knowing he is connecting the past to the future in his very person, handing down through his ministry the great gift that has been received—for which he will one day hear those thrilling words: "Well done, good and faithful servant: because thou hast been faithful over a few things, I will place thee over many things. Enter thou into the joy of thy lord" (Mt 25:21). Indeed, by their perseverance in the face of corrupt religious leaders, such priests will inspire greater sanctity in others and place themselves in the noble company of those first heroes of the Catholic priesthood, who rejoiced to be deemed worthy to suffer for the truth of Christ.[92]

Modern people, heirs of an incoherent totalitarian liberalism, typically oscillate between despising all authority and blindly submitting to whatever authority they still acknowledge. There is no longer a network of authorities at various levels that form a constellation of reference points within which the individual Christian yields his obedience to God and to the hierarchy that proceeds from God.[93] Authority is too often twisted into a voluntaristic, arbitrary caricature of itself, and the obedience given to such a substitute is itself a caricature. It is no virtue to submit to known falsehoods; there is no merit in obeying a system erected on errors and lies.[94] Recall what the great Anglican convert Hugh Ross Williamson wrote in 1970 in his blistering pamphlet *The Great Betrayal*:

True Obedience in the Church

Our bishops, forbidding this rite, call on our "obedience." But they must surely know that obedience to conscience takes precedence of everything, and that obedience cannot be commanded for something wrong. Even in military life, a soldier can no longer plead obedience to a superior as an excuse for committing a crime. What the bishops mean by "obedience" is mindless regimentation—the kind of obedience which the apostate priests of the first Reformation gave to their apostate bishops, among whom there was only one who defended the Faith: St. John Fisher. At the moment, there is no St. John Fisher.

The defense of the Church, in the face of the great betrayal by the ecclesiastics, devolves on the laity, who should be active in pursuing the policy which is already coming into effect in various places —providing a priest to say the Tridentine Mass and devoting to his upkeep all the money they would normally give to their local church. As we are back to the Catacombs, the celebration can be held in private houses.

There can be no possible censures for this. It was for this eventuality that St. Pius decreed: "At no time in the future can a priest ever be forced to use any other way of saying Mass." It would, in the end, be impossible to accuse of schism those who continued to use the form of Mass sanctified by the centuries. It is the ecumenists who would be the schismatics.[95]

Our situation today is both worse than in 1970, in that the depth of the heterodoxy and corruption is worse, and better, in that many more people see it for what it is and have made a resolute return to tradition. We even have in the hierarchy a few bishops of the mettle of St. John Fisher. On that note, I might add that the arguments presented in this tract implicate not only priests but also bishops and cardinals: they, too, are obliged to uphold the indefeasible rights of immemorial tradition and venerable Catholic worship together with the rights of Christ's faithful in all ranks and states of life, and no power on earth, not even the pope's, can relieve them of this responsibility in the sight of God.[96]

It is no virtue to submit to known falsehoods; there is no merit in obeying a system erected on errors and lies.

The available evidence shows that, at the highest levels of the Church, we are dealing with a new "pornocracy," the reign of not a few mean-spirited, mentally dull, petty and vindictive thugs who don't care about theology, history, tradition, canon law, or anything except their own ideology, which is all too often recognizable by its sickly lavender hue. This is why no arguments will prevail with them; no appeals to kindness, fairness, justice, mercy; no petitions even if signed by millions. And that is why they must be opposed with complete and utter refusal to comply with any of their destructive demands. Whatever penalties they issue will be without force, as a future pope or council will recognize. Indeed, refusing to acknowledge the efficacy of unjust penalties, refusing to change one's behavior in response to sophisticated bullying, may be regarded as a demonstration of true and heartfelt charity—a sincere love for the Church's pastors that is not content to allow the custodians of tradition to endanger the salvation of their own souls and the souls of others by abusing their power to the detriment of the sacred treasures committed to their care.

Meanwhile, conscience must do its job and not let itself be extinguished by a specious abuse of obedience, a noble virtue frequently dragged through the mud by its exploiters. In this way we will also add luster to obedience in its highest, most beautiful, most radical form: obedience to the truth, for love of the good—for the love of God.

Further Reading

In order to keep this tract a manageable length, I have had to summarize many complex topics, presenting only the most salient points. For certain readers, it may well raise more questions than it answers. The following books and articles are intended as a guide to acquiring a broader and deeper grasp of the current state of the Catholic Church and of several controversial topics touched on in these pages. The articles mentioned here may be easily found online.

On the state of the Church in general, I highly recommend Bishop Athanasius Schneider's book-length interview *Christus Vincit: Christ's Triumph Over the Darkness of the Age* (Angelico, 2019). His Excellency's overview of modern Church history, the Second Vatican Council, the post-conciliar period, and the pontificate of Francis provides a full context for the arguments contained herein. Bronwen McShea's article "Bishops Unbound" (*First Things*, January 2019) diagnoses one of the root causes of the present meltdown in ecclesiastical life by describing the shift from a once highly differentiated and widespread sharing in Church governance, with a prominent role for laity, to an increasing concentration of all effective authority in the hands of bishops and finally in the hands of the pope who appoints and manages all of them. Together with McShea, one should read "Is It Time to Abolish the USCCB?" by Leila Marie Lawler (*Crisis Magazine*, September 16, 2019), "Hierarchy as Middle Management" by Darrick Taylor (*Crisis Magazine*, September 29, 2021), and "The Divide Between the Bishops and the Faithful" by Eric Sammons (*Crisis Magazine*, October 1, 2021).

Roberto de Mattei's *Love for the Papacy and Filial Resistance to the Pope in the History of the Church* (Angelico, 2019) defends the legitimacy of criticizing, disagreeing with, or opposing Roman pontiffs, citing many historical examples. In the collection of essays *Are Canonizations Infallible? Revisiting a Disputed Question* (Arouca, 2021), various authors engage the nature and limits of papal infallibility and the hot-button issue of the reliability of the "saint factory" of recent decades. On the topic of papal heresy, one may consult Arnaldo Xavier da Silveira's *Can a Pope Be . . . a Heretic? The Theological Hypothesis of a Heretical Pope* (Caminhos Romanos, 2018); the same author's *Can Documents of the Magisterium of the Church Contain Errors?* (The American TFP, 2015) is also worthy of attention, as is chapter 10 of José Antonio Ureta's *Pope Francis's "Paradigm Shift"* (The American TFP, 2018), "It Is Licit to Resist," which has the added benefit of quoting extensively the hyperpapalist views of named acolytes of Bergoglianity, which are truly shocking to read. Unquestionably the most important publication documenting and analyzing the many errors espoused and propounded by Pope Francis is the collection entitled *Defending the Faith Against Present Heresies*, edited by John R.T. Lamont and Claudio Pierantoni (Arouca, 2021).

The notion of obedience has arguably suffered from the influence of Jesuit notions: see John R.T. Lamont, "Tyranny and Sexual Abuse in the Catholic Church: A Jesuit Tragedy," *Rorate Caeli*, October 27, 2018. A fuller version of that article was presented as a lecture in New York City on April 4, 2014, under the title "The Catholic Church and the Rule of Law," the text of which was published on May 8 in two parts at The Society of St. Hugh of Cluny's weblog. Likewise recommended is the pamphlet *Faithful*

Children of the Church: Catholic Obedience in Times of Apostasy (Rome: Lepanto Foundation, 2018; available from Voice of the Family), which contains essays by Roberto de Mattei, Fr. Roger-Thomas Calmel, O.P., and Prof. Plinio Corrêa de Oliveira.

If you are going to read only a single book on the Mass, read Michael Fiedrowicz's *The Traditional Mass: History, Form, and Theology of the Classical Roman Rite* (Angelico, 2020). For an explanation of the Tridentine rite's superiority over the Novus Ordo on every level and in every respect, see my book *Reclaiming Our Roman Catholic Birthright: The Genius and Timeliness of the Traditional Latin Mass* (Angelico, 2020). On the rupture between the old and new rites, see Fr. Raymond Dulac's *In Defence of the Roman Mass* (Te Deum Press, 2020), and, for briefer treatments, my articles "Beyond 'Smells and Bells': Why We Need the Objective Content of the *Usus Antiquior*" (*Rorate Caeli*, November 29, 2019); "Two 'Forms' of the Roman Rite: Liturgical Fact or Canonical Fiat?" (*Rorate Caeli*, September 14, 2020); and "The Byzantine Liturgy, the Traditional Latin Mass, and the Novus Ordo—Two Brothers and a Stranger" (*New Liturgical Movement*, June 4, 2018). Fr. Dulac's book includes detailed treatments of the legal standing of the *Missale Romanum* canonized in perpetuity by St. Pius V in *Quo Primum* and compares it with that of Paul VI's would-be "Roman Missal": see *In Defence of the Roman Mass*, 111–24, 207–10, 219–34, 265–303. Fr. Dulac tends toward a hyperpapalism that I would not share, but this makes his carefully reasoned arguments against the Novus Ordo and against any obligation to use it all the more triumphant.

To understand better the plight of priests who are punished for ideological reasons, see Fr. John P. Lovell, "What is a Canceled Priest?," *OnePeterFive*, October 4, 2021, as well as my article "Discovering Tradition: A Priest's Crisis of Conscience," *OnePeterFive*, March 27, 2019. For a good summary of the internal strife the pontificate of Francis has created for any still-believing Catholic priest, see Fr. Timothy Sauppé's "A Sense of Pastoral Betrayal: The Burden Papal Novelties Lay on Parish Priests," *OnePeterFive*, January 12, 2021. I recommend looking up the Coalition for Canceled Priests.

The attentive reader will have noticed that the endnotes in this booklet frequently cite the anthology *From Benedict's Peace to Francis's War: Catholics Respond to the Motu Proprio* Traditionis Custodes *on the Latin Mass* (Angelico, 2021). This must-have resource gathers seventy of the finest responses to the papal decree, written by forty-five authors from twelve countries.

Endnotes

1 Text available at www.columbia.edu/acis/ets/CCREAD
   /etscc/kant.html.

2 Text available at www.pathsoflove.com/aquinas/perfection
   -of-the-spiritual-life.html.

3 We must nevertheless be careful about how we interpret and
   apply the teaching of such masters in the present day. See
   my article "Sun, Moon, and Stars: Tradition for the Saints,"
   OnePeterFive, February 3, 2021. The spiritual advice given
   by some of the saints in the past (which often amounts to
   "submit without a whimper to everything your superior does/
   commands") rested on assumptions that such saints could
   take for granted: a common assent to Catholic dogma, respect for ecclesiastical tradition, veneration for the inherited

liturgy, acceptance of the role of fine art, etc. Today, one is fortunate if one can assume elementary faith in Christ the Redeemer!

The historical context within which we are trying to understand and live the virtue of obedience cannot be ignored. We should not take advice from three or four or fifteen centuries ago, typically directed at consecrated religious in the state of vowed obedience, and apply it to ourselves as if it were a stencil or a cookie-cutter and we were blank paper or dough. If, for example, one's superior is a modernist, then one has to use discernment about which commands are not contaminated with or derived from his modernism, and which ones are. (In a case of doubt, one would have to make a judgment about what is more probable.) Whoever gave "blind obedience" to a superior who is known to be a liberal, progressive, or modernist would *ipso facto* sin against faith, against truth, and against the charity that loves God first and above all else.

It is true that one may accept an injustice to oneself as an act of redemptive suffering; but one is not allowed to watch injustices being done to others and let it happen (if it is within one's power to prevent it or in some way to intervene), and above all we are not allowed to let Our Lord be treated unfittingly or contemptuously (think of the maltreatment of the Blessed Sacrament in so many churches and liturgies!).

When the rights of God are at stake, one may not "offer up" the evil and turn away, much less endorse it or practice it.

4   On the anthropological and liturgical implications of Christ as the Eternal High Priest and the Church's ministers as His visible instruments, see my book *Ministers of Christ: Recovering the Roles of Clergy and Laity in an Age of Confusion* (Manchester, NH: Crisis Publications, 2021).

5   Conversely, if you take away obedience, you will obscure the permanence and objectivity of the good loved and will undermine commitment to it; if you take away obedience, you will deny the sovereign rights of truth over your mind.

6   This teaching is found in its clearest form in the writings of St. John. See Jn 14:15–21: "If you love me, keep my commandments. And I will ask the Father, and he shall give you another Paraclete, that he may abide with you for ever. The spirit of truth, whom the world cannot receive, because it seeth him not, nor knoweth him: but you shall know him; because he shall abide with you, and shall be in you. I will not leave you orphans, I will come to you. Yet a little while: and the world seeth me no more. But you see me: because I live, and you shall live. In that day you shall know, that I am in my Father, and you in me, and I in you. He that hath my commandments, and keepeth them; he it is that loveth me. And he that loveth me, shall be loved of my Father: and I will love him, and will manifest myself to him." Jn 15:14:

"You are my friends, if you do the things that I command you." See also 1 Jn 2:3–6 and 3:23–24.

7 James Butler, "The Most Rev. Dr. James Butler's Catechism," in *The Tradivox Catholic Catechism Index*, ed. Aaron Seng (Manchester, NH: Sophia Institute Press, 2021), 4:46–47.

8 As St. Thomas maintains, the virtue of prudence is involved in any free action whatsoever. The reason we do not always notice that we are making a prudential judgment about a proposed course of action is that very often it occurs as quick as a flash — if, for example, the thing we are ordered to do is a small matter about which no deliberation is necessary, or if we enjoy such a good working relationship with another person that we habitually do what he says, without pausing to think it through. Nevertheless, there *is* a rational "processing" of any command or request on the basis of which we see it to be something we can and ought to do, even if we might *notice* this prudential reasoning only when there's a hitch that gives us pause.

9 The motives of a superior do not have to be virtuous in order for his commands to be worthy of obedience. For example, a bishop could move a priest from one parish to another out of irritation with his popularity or envy at his success or because he'll be able to fundraise more money for the diocese in a place otherwise not suited to him. These administrative decisions would normally need to be accepted, even if their less-than-admirable motives were apparent or suspected. I only maintain

that there should be no evidence or well-founded suspicion that the superior's decisions are targeted at the spiritual or physical destruction of the subordinate or of the local or universal Church. This is the minimum goodwill presupposed by a viable structure of authority and obedience.

10 As St. Thomas explains: "Wherefore by actions also, especially if they be repeated, so as to make a custom, law can be changed and expounded; and also something can be established which obtains force of law, in so far as by repeated external actions, the inward movement of the will and concepts of reason are most effectually declared; for when a thing is done again and again, it seems to proceed from a deliberate judgment of reason. Accordingly, custom has the force of a law, abolishes law, and is the interpreter of law" (*Summa theologiae* [*ST*] I-II, Q. 97, art. 3). For further explanation, see "The Legality of the Old Rite" at *The Rad Trad*, October 25, 2018.

11 This is no mere theoretical point. It seems that Pope Francis has flagrantly lied about the results of the bishops' survey on *Summorum Pontificum*. See Diane Montagna, "*Traditionis Custodes*: Separating Fact from Fiction," *The Remnant*, October 7, 2021.

12 As Massimo Viglione memorably states: "Obedience— and this is an error that finds its deepest roots even in the preconciliar Church, it must be said—is not an end. It is a means of sanctification. Therefore, it is not an absolute value, but rather an instrumental one. It is a positive value, very

positive, if it is ordered toward God. But if one obeys Satan, or his servants, or error, or apostasy, then obedience is no longer a good, but rather a deliberate participation in evil" ("'They Will Throw You out of the Synagogues' [Jn 16:2]: The Hermeneutic of Cain's Envy against Abel," in *From Benedict's Peace to Francis's War: Catholics Respond to the Motu Proprio* Traditionis Custodes *on the Latin Mass* [Brooklyn, NY: Angelico Press, 2021], 110).

13 "The Virtue of Obedience," *First Things* online, July 23, 2021. My citing of Chaput is not intended as blanket approval of his pastoral decisions (see, e.g., Michael Davies, *Liturgical Time Bombs in Vatican II* [Rockford, IL: TAN Books, 2003], 52–54).

14 See *ST* II-II, Q. 104, art. 1. See, inter alia, Leo XIII, *Diuturnum Illud* 11 and 17; *Immortale Dei* 18; *Libertas Praestantissimum* 13.

15 See *ST* II-II, QQ. 104 and 105.

16 *ST* II-II, Q. 104, art. 5, sed contra.

17 Ibid., corpus.

18 Ibid., ad 2.

19 Ibid., ad 3.

20 *ST* II-II, Q. 105, art. 2.

21 As so often in his social encyclicals, Leo XIII is restating here the doctrine of St. Thomas Aquinas in the treatise on law: see, e.g., *ST* I-II, Q. 96.

22 I owe the insights and some of the language of the next few paragraphs to Dr. Jeremy Holmes, whom I cordially

thank. For a fuller account of the points made here, see his post "How formal authority works," *New Song*, October 21, 2021, http://drandmrsholmes.com/blog/2021/10/21/how-authority-works-2/.

23 Tragically, the term "common good," like "obedience" and "conscience," has been so abused in recent decades that it can now come across as a suspicious phrase — something that sounds liberal or progressive. For example, someone might claim that the Church's "common good" requires "having a common worship," i.e., only one Roman Missal (on which spurious claim, see the writings of Joseph Shaw in *From Benedict's Peace to Francis's War*, 260–79, 310–13, and 337–40). We must resist this kind of linguistic thievery and insist on giving terms their correct traditional meaning; we must "combat novelties of words," as Pope St. Pius X exhorted in the great anti-Modernist encyclical *Pascendi Dominici Gregis*. As regards the concept of the "common good," see the explanations given by P. Edmund Waldstein, "The Good, the Highest Good, and the Common Good" and Peter A. Kwasniewski, "The Foundations of Christian Ethics and Social Order," in *Integralism and the Common Good: Selected Essays from "The Josias,"* vol. 1: *Family, City, and State* (Brooklyn, NY: Angelico Press, 2021), 7–48, especially 22–30 and 39–46.

24 In the post mentioned two notes above, Dr. Holmes draws the following conclusion: "The authority's decree only binds because a person's reason can perceive the weight of the

common good behind it. If that decree is destructive of the common good in a way that the person's reason cannot be uncertain about, then the decree loses all moral force. Obedience is always rooted in reason's grasp of the good. It is not arbitrary or blind."

25 For additional argumentation in support of this thesis, see my lecture "Beyond 'Smells and Bells': Why We Need the Objective Content of the *Usus Antiquior*," *Rorate Caeli*, November 29, 2019.

26 *The Liturgical Year*, vol. 1: *Advent*, trans. Dom Laurence Shepherd (Great Falls, MT: St. Bonaventure Publications, 2000), 1–2, 8, 16, emphasis added.

27 *John Henry Newman on Worship, Reverence, and Ritual: A Selection of Texts*, ed. Peter A. Kwasniewski (n.p.: Os Justi Press, 2019), 442.

28 See "The Problem of False Antiquarianism" in my book *Reclaiming Our Roman Catholic Birthright* (Brooklyn, NY: Angelico Press, 2020), 149–60. In any case, antiquarianism was no more than a convenient excuse for the modernist liturgical reformers, since, as it turned out, they abolished or diluted many indisputably ancient elements of the Roman Rite, heavily redacted the ancient sources they took up, and introduced plenty of sheer novelties that could be passed off as "something like what the early Christians must have done." Nothing has been more fraudulent or mendacious than the post-conciliar appeal to antiquity.

Endnotes

29 *Concilii Vaticani II Synopsis in ordinem redigens schemata cum relationibus necnon Patrum orationes atque animadversiones. Constitutio de Sacra Liturgia Sacrosanctum Concilium*, ed. Francisco Gil Hellín (Città del Vaticano: Libreria Editrice Vaticana, 2003), 828.

30 *The Holy Sacrifice of the Mass Dogmatically, Liturgically, and Ascetically Explained* (St. Louis: Herder, 1949), 261.

31 Gihr, *Holy Sacrifice*, 581.

32 It belongs to divine law that the faithful should worship in rites handed down from God, from the Church, from holy men and women. We see this principle in both the Old Testament (e.g., "Look and make it according to the pattern that was shewn thee in the mount," Ex 25:40; "Pass not beyond the ancient bounds which thy fathers have set," Prov 22:28) and in the New Testament ("I delivered unto you first of all that which also I received," 1 Cor 15:3 [KJV]; "Stand fast; and hold the traditions which you have learned, whether by word, or by our epistle," 2 Thess 2:14). Those who point to the distinction between "primary and secondary" or "essential and accidental" elements often greatly misconstrue it, failing to recognize how it actually supports tradition rather than pushing it aside as nugatory. I have discussed this issue many times; see, e.g., the chapter "The Charge of Aestheticism" in *Reclaiming Our Roman Catholic Birthright*, 193–204, and my article "How Much Can the Pope Change Our Rites, and Why Would He?," *OnePeterFive*, October 20, 2021.

33 *From Benedict's Peace to Francis's War*, 104–5.

34 See "An Interview with His Excellency Bishop Vitus Huonder," at sspx.org, under News and Events, October 1, 2021. Elsewhere in the same interview he states: "The Faith is given, it is also over all authority, or rather all authority is subject to the authority of the Faith, which ultimately means subject to the authority of Our Lord, because the Faith comes from Our Lord. And all authority must answer to Him.... I repeat: the Faith is given by Our Lord, through the Apostles who transmitted it, and this Faith binds us. Now, this is what, in large part, is missing today in the Church, and [this is] what threatens unity."

35 Adrian Fortescue, "Liturgy of the Mass," *The Catholic Encyclopedia*, special ed. (New York: The Encyclopedia Press, 1913), 9:800.

36 For more on this point, see my article "Surprising Convergences between an Anti-Catholic Textbook and the Liturgical Reform," *New Liturgical Movement*, August 5, 2019.

37 "From *Summorum Pontificum* to *Traditionis Custodes*, or From the Reserve to the Zoo," at fsspx.news, July 19, 2021.

38 An extensive treatment of this topic may be found in my lecture "The Pope's Boundedness to Tradition as a Legislative Limit," in *From Benedict's Peace to Francis's War*, 222–47.

39 For the full text of the Oath in Latin and in English, see "'I Shall Keep Inviolate the Discipline and Ritual of the Church': The Early Mediæval Papal Oath," *Canticum Salomonis*, July 31, 2021.

40 Suárez, *De Fide*, disp. X, sect. VI, n. 16. The reader should be aware that Suárez and others who speak in similar terms were reacting to the Protestant *mischaracterization* of an absolutist papal authority that ironically became commonplace among Catholics after Vatican I.

41 *De Caritate*, disp. XII, sect. 1: "si nollet tenere cum toto Ecclesiae corpore unionem et conjunctionem quam debet, ut si tentaret totam Ecclesiam excommunicare, aut si vellet omnes ecclesiasticas caeremonias apostolica traditione firmatas evertere." It is important to note here that, when it comes to the oldest elements of liturgical rites, we often have no way of knowing (and may never have the ability to know) which of these are of merely ecclesiastical institution and which are of divine, apostolic, or subapostolic institution — which makes it all the more crucial not to eliminate any of them. The wisdom of several nineteenth-century bishops, in explaining the invalidity of Anglican orders, may here be invoked. After having said that local or regional Churches could and did *add* to the liturgy for its enrichment or embellishment, they observe: "That they were also permitted to *subtract* prayers and ceremonies in previous use, and even to remodel the existing rites in the most drastic manner, is a proposition for which we know of no historical foundation, and which appears to us absolutely incredible. ... Adhering rigidly to the rite handed down to us we can always feel secure; whereas, if we omit or change

anything, we may perhaps be abandoning just that element which is essential." See *A Vindication of the Bull "Apostolicæ Curæ"* (London: Longmans, Green, and Co., 1898), 44, 42.

42 Athanasius, *Encyclical Letter*, trans. M. Atkinson and Archibald Robertson, *Nicene and Post-Nicene Fathers*, Second Series, vol. 4, ed. Philip Schaff and Henry Wace (Buffalo, NY: Christian Literature Publishing Co., 1892), rev. and ed. for *New Advent* by Kevin Knight, my emphasis added. By "forms" Athanasius is referring to the public customs of prayer and worship, the *lex orandi*.

43 In the memorable words of St. Vincent of Lérins's *Commonitory*, ch. 3, n. 7: "What [will a Catholic Christian do], if some novel contagion seek to infect not merely an insignificant portion of the Church, but the whole? Then it will be his care to cleave to antiquity, which at this day cannot possibly be seduced by any fraud of novelty" (trans. C.A. Heurtley, *Nicene and Post-Nicene Fathers*, Second Series, vol. 11, ed. Philip Schaff and Henry Wace [Buffalo, NY: Christian Literature Publishing Co., 1894], rev. and ed. for *New Advent* by Kevin Knight). The inherited Roman liturgy is *known with certainty* to be fully and authentically Catholic. The same certainty cannot be extended to the products of Annibale Bugnini's Consilium, with their outrageous novelties and arbitrary archaeologisms. Critics of the Latin Mass have argued that some of its most familiar customs, such as receiving Communion on the tongue while kneeling, represent a departure from

the "tradition" practiced earlier and therefore undermine the claim that this Mass is the most traditional. This is no serious argument. The later customs emerged logically from the earlier customs by following out their implications: thus, a more intense focus on the mystery of transubstantiation and the Real Presence led to ever-greater signs of reverence. The tradition was not overturned but deepened, as the Church progressed from a *good* way of doing or saying something to a *better* way — better either absolutely (as with kneeling to receive on the tongue, which in the West is a sign of adoration and humility), or better relative to legitimate pastoral concerns (as with communicating under the species of bread alone). Vincent's appeal to antiquity, so far from being a simplistic appeal to a random historical moment, takes into account the logical consequences of the Church's faith.

44 *Mitre & Crook* (Brooklyn, NY: Angelico Press, 2019), 117.

45 *From Benedict's Peace to Francis's War*, 220. Fr. John Hunwicke comments: "The Catholic Church, more than many ecclesial bodies, has a deeply ingrained sense of Law. This makes it easy for Roman Catholics to underestimate the force of *auctoritas* [i.e., the authority inherent in something enjoying long-lasting and widespread acceptance]. But Benedict XVI was appealing directly to *auctoritas* when he wrote: 'What earlier generations held as sacred, remains sacred and great for us too, and it cannot be all of a sudden entirely forbidden or even considered harmful'" (ibid., 33).

46 "On the Credibility of the Catholic Church," in *From Bene-dict's Peace to Francis's War*, 296; the internal quotation is from Benedict XVI's Letter to Bishops of July 7, 2007.

47 See my article "Does *Traditionis Custodes* Lack Juridical Stand-ing?," *From Benedict's Peace to Francis's War*, 74–78.

48 *From Benedict's Peace to Francis's War*, 168.

49 See Joseph Shaw, "St. Pius V and the Mass," *Voice of the Family*, October 6, 2021.

50 "St. Pius V did not create a new set of liturgical books but codi-fied as carefully as possible the historical practice of the Church of Rome, a *lex orandi* fully expressive of the Catholic Faith that was then under attack by the Protestants. He solemnly established this rite of Mass as a *regula fidei* by his Apostolic Constitution *Quo Primum* of July 14, 1570. This Bull was republished in subsequent editions of the missal by his papal successors, as a sign of continuity in the *lex orandi*, precisely so that the *lex credendi* might be fully preserved and handed down" ("Does *Traditionis Custodes* Lack Juridical Standing?," in *From Benedict's Peace to Francis's War*, 75). A merely disciplin-ary decree supplants its earlier equivalents by the very fact of being published, which explains why a new document of this type would never reproduce the content of the *earlier* decree it replaces. The argument that sees *Quo Primum* as moral and dogmatic was advanced and defended by Fr. Gregory Hesse; for a summary, see Michael Baker, "The Status of the *Novus Ordo Missae*," *Super Flumina Babylonis*, February 21, 2021. My

citation of Baker's essay does not mean I agree with all of his conclusions, as neither would I agree with all of Hesse's.

51 Pius V, *Quo Primum*; the text is taken from *Papal Encyclicals Online*, as it is not posted at the Vatican's website. It should be noted that exactly the same argument as the one concerning the *Missale Romanum* can and must be made about all of the traditional rites and ceremonies contained in the *Rituale Romanum* and in the *Pontificale Romanum*. All of them are the authentic *lex orandi* of the Roman Church, expressing her *lex credendi*.

52 There are those who say "Oh, that's just papal boilerplate language, which you can find in all sorts of documents that establish things later overturned."

Yes — and no. One must look not only at the language, but at the nature of the things to which the language points. To say such-and-such a disciplinary law must never be altered would not prevent a future pope with equal authority from modifying it; but in *Quo Primum* we are dealing with more than discipline: we are dealing with the transmission of the Church's faith in its most ancient, most authoritative, most normative form, which takes precedence over the Magisterium itself. Why would St. Pius V describe a liturgical rite in such repeated, emphatic, and solemn language, if he had no intention of conveying that this rite *is* the liturgical expression of the Roman Church's faith of all time, for all time? Obviously that does not exclude additions such as the feast of Christ the King, minor modifications such as elevating or reducing a particular saint's rank in the calendar, or changes in keeping with the trajectory of devotion such as kneeling rather than standing for Holy Communion, but it surely renders impossible the idea of abolishing an immemorial rite altogether, or "modifying" it to such an extent that the end result amounts to its repudiation (see the devastating article by Matthew Hazell, "'All the Elements of the Roman Rite'? Mythbusting, Part II," *New Liturgical Movement*, October 1, 2021).

This is why the inclusion of the new Holy Week of Pius XII in the 1962 *editio typica* of the *Missale Romanum* causes that missal to be in contradiction with its prefatory *Quo Primum*, which the Pacellian Holy Week implicitly defies, inasmuch as it is a rupture from Catholic Tradition and therefore a sin against God's liturgical Providence. Traditionalists who seek to be consistent with their principles must utilize the pre-55 Holy Week, for which no permission is necessary. For historical background, see my articles "Coincidences during the reign of Pius XII? Political background to Vatican II and liturgical changes" (*LifeSiteNews*, May 25, 2021) and "Lights and Shadows in the Pontificate of Pius XII" (*OnePeterFive*, September 22, 2021).

53 See the Bull *Iniunctum Nobis* of 1564 issued by Pius V's predecessor, Pius IV.

54 For a full-scale defense, see my lecture mentioned earlier in note 25, "Beyond Smells and Bells," as well as the lectures

"Two 'Forms' of the Roman Rite: Liturgical Fact or Canonical Fiat?" (*Rorate Caeli*, September 14, 2020) and "Beyond *Summorum Pontificum*: The Work of Retrieving the Tridentine Heritage" (*Rorate Caeli*, July 14, 2021).

55 In an interview with Carlos Herrera on Radio COPE, Francis said: "After this motu proprio, a priest who wants to celebrate that is not in the same condition as before — that it was for nostalgia, for desire, &c.— and so he has to ask permission from Rome. A kind of permission for bi-ritualism, which is given only by Rome. [Like] a priest who celebrates in the Eastern Rite and the Latin Rite, he is bi-ritual but with the permission of Rome" (transcript here: www.vaticannews.va/en/pope/news/2021-09/pope-after-operation-it-never-crossed-my-mind-to-resign.html). In a conversation with Jesuits in Slovakia he said: "From now on those who want to celebrate with the *vetus ordo* must ask permission from [*sic*] as is done with biritualism" (transcript here: www.laciviltacattolica.com/freedom-scares-us-pope-francis-conversation-with-slovak-jesuits/).

56 Bishop Schneider puts it bluntly: "The increasing spread of celebrations of the Traditional Mass reveals to all that there is—upon honest and closer examination—a real break between the two rites both ritually and doctrinally. The traditional rite is, so to speak, a constant reproach to the authorities of the Holy See, saying: 'You have made a revolution in the liturgy.'" Translated from "Entretien exclusif

de Mgr. Athanasius Schneider à MPI," *Médias-Presse-Info*, September 24, 2021.

57 The new missal of Pope Paul VI bears alarming similarities to Cranmer's rite, as may be readily observed in any dispassionate comparison. Charts useful for this purpose can be found at www.whispersofrestoration.com/chart and www.lms.org.uk/missals.

58 William Lilly, "England (Since the Reformation)," *The Catholic Encyclopedia*, special ed. (New York: The Encyclopedia Press, 1913), 5:449. For a detailed and eye-opening account of the liturgical revolution in sixteenth-century England, see Michael Davies, *Cranmer's Godly Order: The Destruction of Catholicism through Liturgical Change*, rev. ed. (Ft. Collins, CO: Roman Catholic Books, 1995).

59 "*Sensus Fidei* in the Life of the Church," nn. 61–62. The document is available at the Vatican website.

60 Ibid., n. 63. The document cites additional texts by St. Thomas Aquinas that are worthy of much consideration. For further commentary, see Roberto de Mattei, "Resistance and Fidelity to the Church in Times of Crisis," in idem, *Love for the Papacy and Filial Resistance to the Pope in the History of the Church* (Brooklyn: Angelico Press, 2019), 105–30. Sadly, as is so typical of Vatican documents nowadays, the penultimate paragraph (§127) is a nauseating paean to the "new Pentecost" of the Second Vatican Council and the "new ways" of Pope Francis. Even the good Homer nods off from time to time.

61 See John Clark, "Without the Right of Conscience, There Is No Common Good," *Crisis Magazine*, September 28, 2021. As Rubén Peretó Rivas says: "There is a general principle of natural law that applies to any authority: commands must be rational. If a command is not ordered by reason, it is not law but force and violence. And while the pope cannot be judged by anyone on earth, his manifestly irrational laws or commands can be resisted. For example, even if the pope did not like people of color, he could not suppress the African dioceses; nor could he ordain all the males of his family bishops to give luster to the Bergoglios. If he does not like kibbeh and sfiha, he could not suppress the Maronite rite; and we could give other examples of irrationalities that a pope could not do—in regard to which, were he to do them, it would be licit, if not obligatory, to resist him" (*From Benedict's Peace to Francis's War*, 294).

62 John Henry Newman, *Arians of the Fourth Century*, Note 5: The Orthodoxy of the Body of the Faithful during the Supremacy of Arianism (www.newmanreader.org/works/arians /note5.html). For further reading, see Cardinal Walter Brandmüller's lecture "On Consulting the Faithful in Matters of Doctrine," given April 7, 2018 in Rome (full text at www. lifesitenews.com/news/cardinal-brandmueller-talk/).

63 The words of Archbishop Carlo Maria Viganò are moving in their honesty: "I confess it with serenity and without controversy: I was one of the many people who, despite

many perplexities and fears which today have proven to be absolutely legitimate, trusted the authority of the hierarchy with unconditional obedience. In reality, I think that many people, including myself, did not initially consider the possibility that there could be a conflict between obedience to an order of the hierarchy and fidelity to the Church herself. What made tangible this unnatural, indeed I would even say perverse, separation between the hierarchy and the Church, between obedience and fidelity, was certainly this most recent pontificate" (*A Voice in the Wilderness*, ed. Brian M. McCall [Brooklyn, NY: Angelico Press, 2021], 175). Massimo Viglione puts his finger on a weakness in some "traditionalist" circles: "The first concern ought to be to always follow and defend the Truth, not the cloying, obsequious, and scrupulous groveling which is the spoiled fruit of a misunderstood Tridentinism" (*From Benedict's Peace to Francis's War*, 110–11).

64 *ST* I, Q. 79, art. 13.

65 From "Letter to the Duke of Norfolk," quoted in *Catechism of the Catholic Church* (New York: Doubleday, 1995), 1778 [hereafter CCC].

66 *Gaudium et Spes* 16, quoted in CCC 1776.

67 Quoted in CCC 1779.

68 CCC 1777, emphasis added.

69 *Commentary on John*, trans. J. Weisheipl and F. Larcher (Albany: Magi Books, 1980), ch. 7, lec. 5, n. 1090.

70 See Marc D. Guerra, "Thomas More's Correspondence on Conscience," *Religion & Liberty*, vol. 10, n. 6, July 20, 2010, www.acton.org/thomas-mores-correspondence-conscience. In his *Commentary on the Sentences*, St. Thomas says (*In IV Sent.*, Dist. 38, Q. 2, art. 4, qa. 3) that a married man must be ready to die excommunicate rather than have marital relations with someone whom a church tribunal decrees to be his wife, but whom he knows is not his wife, since "truthfulness of life … must not be given up [even] to avoid scandal."

71 For an excellent Thomistic discussion of conscience, how it interacts with God's law, why it must be followed, and how it can be stifled or perverted, see J. Budziszewski, *What We Can't Not Know: A Guide*, rev. ed. (San Francisco: Ignatius Press, 2011). See also the profound address by the late Cardinal Carlo Caffarra, "The Restoration of Man," published at *The Catholic World Report*, September 20, 2017. An excerpt: "Conscience says absolutely: you have to do this action; you mustn't do that action. The voice of conscience confronts man's freedom with an absolute: an absolute duty…. Man cannot dispense himself from an obligation which the judgement of conscience forces on him: the universal experience of remorse proves it…. The fact that man feels he cannot dispense himself from an obligation dictated by his own conscience shows that its judgment makes the person know a truth that pre-exists conscience itself. A truth, that

is, which is not true because our conscience knows it, but, vice-versa; our conscience knows it because that truth exists. In other words: it is not truth that depends on conscience, but conscience that depends on truth."

72 In the words of Fr. John Hunwicke: "No *auctoritas* can subsist in enactments which manifestly subvert Holy Tradition" (*From Benedict's Peace to Francis's War*, 32).

73 *ST* I-II, Q. 96, art. 4. Inasmuch as "disobedience" names a vice, the refusal to follow an unjust law should not be called "disobedience" *simpliciter*. As Fr. Francisco José Delgado explains: "The pope cannot change Tradition by decree or say that the post-Vatican II liturgy is the only expression of the *lex orandi* in the Roman Rite. Since this is false, the legislation stemming from this principle is invalid and, according to Catholic morals, should not be observed, which does not imply disobedience." Quoted in José Antonio Ureta, "The Faithful Are Entitled to Defend Themselves against Liturgical Aggression," in *From Benedict's Peace to Francis's War*, 168.

74 Roberto de Mattei, "2021 in the Light of the Fatima Message and Right Reason," *Rorate Caeli*, January 2, 2021.

75 Sebastian Morello, "Revolution and Repudiation: Governance Gone Awry," in *From Benedict's Peace to Francis's War*, 99. Similarly, Bishop Schneider writes: "An almost one-thousand-year-old valid and highly esteemed liturgical treasure is not the private property of a pope, which he can

freely dispose of. Therefore, seminarians and young priests must ask for the right to use this common treasure of the Church, and should they be denied this right, they can use it nevertheless, perhaps in a clandestine manner. This would not be an act of disobedience, but rather of obedience to Holy Mother Church, who has given us this liturgical treasure. The firm rejection of an almost one-thousand-year-old liturgical form by Pope Francis represents, in fact, a short-lived phenomenon compared to the constant spirit and praxis of the Church" ("A Drastic and Tragic Act," in *From Benedict's Peace to Francis's War*, 147). In a conference in Paris on June 25, 2021, Bishop Schneider did not hesitate to declare: "The faithful and the priests have the right to a liturgy that is the liturgy of all the saints.... In consequence the Holy See does not have the power to suppress a heritage of the whole Church. That would be an abuse, even on the part of bishops. In this case, you can continue to celebrate the Mass in this form: it is a form of obedience ... to all the popes who have celebrated this Mass" (quoted by Jean-Pierre Maugendre, "Francis: The Pope of Exclusion," in *From Benedict's Peace to Francis's War*, 62).

76 Archbishop Viganò has some good advice about navigating the situation: "The response to any limitation or prohibition of the celebration of the traditional Mass must obviously take into account both the objective elements and the different situations: if a priest has as an Ordinary a sworn enemy of

the ancient rite who has no qualms about suspending him *a divinis* if he were to celebrate the Tridentine Mass, public disobedience could be a way to make the abuse of the Ordinary clear, especially if the news is spread by the media: the Prelates are very afraid of media coverage about their actions, and sometimes they prefer to refrain from canonical measures just to avoid ending up in the newspapers. The priest must therefore consider whether his action will be more effective with a fair and direct confrontation, or by acting with discretion and in hiding. In my opinion, the first option is the most linear and transparent, and the one that responds most to the behavior of the Saints, to which we must comply" ("*Lapides Clamabunt,*" in *From Benedict's Peace to Francis's War*, 203–4).

77 It should be noted in this connection that both Cardinal Josyf Slipyj and Cardinal Karol Wojtyła performed secret ordinations because of their inner conviction that the good of the Church behind the Iron Curtain required it; Archbishop Marcel Lefebvre offered the same defense of his own dramatic (albeit public) step. See my article "Clandestine Ordinations Against Church Law: Lessons from Cardinal Wojtyła and Cardinal Slipyj," *OnePeterFive*, October 13, 2021.

78 See Fr. John P. Lovell, "What Is a Canceled Priest?," *OnePeterFive*, October 4, 2021. Let me emphasize: I am speaking about a priest who is punished for *nothing other than* the "fault" of

adherence to liturgical tradition, which is not a fault but a resplendent virtue — for example, a priest who is suspended just for continuing to say the traditional Latin Mass after the local Ordinary has dared to forbid it; or a priest who is removed from his pastorship and any parochial duties because he can no longer, in good conscience, distribute Holy Communion in the hand. Invariably, most superiors in cases like this will devise trumped-up charges to distract from the real issue.

The principle of "what is freely given can be freely taken away" must be properly understood. No man has an absolute right to become a priest, and no priest has an absolute right to offer the Mass or celebrate the other sacraments. But if we understand that the very purpose of the priesthood is to offer sacrifice, to reconcile sinners, to add new members to the Church, etc., then it would be absurd, once a man is ordained a priest, to impede his ministry — that is, *Christ's* ministry in and through him — unless he is actually guilty of wrongdoing (e.g., heresy, schism, sexual abuse). It would thus be more accurate to say: "what is freely given for X purpose should not be taken away unless X is violated," or, spelled out more fully, "what is freely given for the common good of the Church and the good of each of Christ's faithful may not be taken away unless the recipient of that gift acts against the common good or against the good of the faithful." This brings us squarely back to the question of the Church's *bonum commune*, which cannot be severed from (in the words of Pius IV, speaking of the traditional Roman Rite) "the received and approved ceremonies of the Catholic Church in the solemn administration of all the sacraments."

79 The conventional line of argument would be that if a priest's faculties have been removed, he may continue to validly (but illicitly) offer the Holy Mass, baptize, confer the Last Rites, and confirm (if he does so at the time of Baptism or reception into the Church), but could not give valid sacramental absolution except in a case of emergency and could not serve as witness to a valid sacramental marriage. Without wishing to deny that there are complicated canonical issues involved, we must not fail to acknowledge the elephant in the room: the traditional Catholic Faith is under unprecedented assault from the very ones who should be its primary upholders and defenders. This already creates a generalized emergency that does not need to be "declared" as such. (Who would declare it? Surely not the lavender modernists who are in positions of highest authority and who benefit from, or at least approve of, the dissolution of Catholic faith and morals.) The fundamental right of the baptized to a traditional sacramental life, being of divine law, may never be compromised by any appeal to or application of human laws, howsoever authoritative they may be *in se*. The law does not provide for every situation, and without a doubt the canonical principles of equity and *epikeia* must

come into play. Canon law exists to facilitate the glorification of God and the sanctification of His people, not to create impediments and obstructions to them. For further reasoning in support of this position, see my article "Have There Been Worse Crises Than This One?," *OnePeterFive*, January 13, 2021.

80 See Roberto de Mattei, *Love for the Papacy and Filial Resistance to the Pope*, 17–22.

81 *Voice in the Wilderness*, 253. Again: "The cancellation of the past and of Tradition, the denial of roots, the delegitimization of dissent, the abuse of authority and the apparent respect for rules: are not these the recurring elements of all dictatorships?" (ibid., 229).

82 *From Benedict's Peace to Francis's War*, 199–200. Of the "conservative" clergy who might try to get by with a "reverent Novus Ordo," Massimo Viglione rightly says: "In the end, sooner or later, even those priests will find themselves at the crossroads of having to choose between obedience to evil or disobedience to evil in order to remain faithful to the Good. The comb of the Revolution, in society as in the Church, does not leave any knots." See my article "Why Restricting the TLM Harms Every Parish Mass," *From Benedict's Peace to Francis's War*, 287–91.

83 As Martin Mosebach said in an interview on October 4, 2021: "The hostility of the present ruling circles in the Church against tradition is unconditional—they will not rest until

tradition is completely destroyed. Pope Francis apparently said the other day: 'Tradition is killing us.' He does not know how right he is: Yes, tradition will sit in judgment over him sooner or later, because it is the essence of the Church, because it is also the basis of the papacy, which does not exist without Tradition" (Maike Hickson, "'Legitimate illegality': Famed Catholic author on how to defend tradition," *LifeSiteNews*, October 4, 2021). We should have the clear-sightedness to recognize that the papacy is undergoing a cancerous mutation right now, not in such a way that the office will be destroyed (for that would be impossible), but in such a way that it is perverting itself in practice, and acting contrary to its own function in the Mystical Body. The motu proprio *Traditionis Custodes* is manifestly an attack on the patrimony of the Church and on its common good. This means that obedience to *this* pope in regard to *these* matters would be disobedience to Christ and to the papacy as such. That is why, even while holding fast to the necessary criterion of communion with Rome, practical choices motivated by legitimate self-defense and proportionate resistance to grave evils may bear a resemblance to the steps that were taken by Archbishop Lefebvre and have been taken by the Society of St. Pius X.

84 *From Benedict's Peace to Francis's War*, 161. In 1998, the Congregation for the Doctrine of the Faith published a reflection entitled "The Primacy of the Successor of Peter

in the Mystery of the Church" (available at the Vatican website), which underlines several key points: "The Roman Pontiff—like all the faithful—is subject to the Word of God, to the Catholic faith.... In other words, the *episkope* of the primacy has limits set by divine law and by the Church's divine, inviolable constitution found in Revelation.... Since the power of the primacy is supreme, there is no other authority to which the Roman Pontiff must juridically answer for his exercise of the gift he has received: '*prima sedes a nemine iudicatur*' [the first See is judged by no one]. This does not mean, however, that the Pope has absolute power.... The ultimate and absolute responsibility of the Pope is best guaranteed, on the one hand, by its relationship to Tradition and fraternal communion and, on the other, by trust in the assistance of the Holy Spirit who governs the Church" (nn. 7 and 10). This last phrase brings us right back to the discussion, above, of the normativity of Tradition and the tradition-sustaining role of the Holy Spirit in the history of the Church, especially in the organic development of her liturgy.

85 State control over ecclesiastical functions was proscribed in Pope Pius IX's *Syllabus of Errors* (1864), which condemned the proposition: "The civil authority may interfere in matters relating to religion ... [and] has the right to make enactments regarding the administration of the divine sacraments, and the dispositions necessary for receiving them" (n. 44).

The fact that clergy likewise may not withhold Mass or the Sacraments from otherwise well-disposed Catholic faithful is a long-established principle in Canon Law (see CIC [1983] 213–214, 384, 519, 528.2), although it has recently become a topic of debate. For the reasonable and faith-filled perspective of a bishop on this matter, I recommend Diane Montagna's interview at *The Remnant* of March 27, 2020, "Bishop Athanasius Schneider on Church's Handling of Coronavirus."

86 From the interview mentioned in the preceding note.

87 The recently widespread prohibitions of Mass in the name of a "public health crisis" are not only unprecedented in Church history, they also belie a dangerously Protestant conception of the Mass. As defined by the Council of Trent, the primary end of Mass is not to serve as a social function or communal meal for the benefit of attendees (though it serves those ends as well), but rather to be a *divine monument*, "a visible sacrifice, such as the nature of man requires, whereby that bloody sacrifice once to be accomplished on the cross might be represented, the memory thereof remain even unto the end of the world, and its salutary effects applied to the remission of those sins which we daily commit" (see *The Canons and Decrees of the Council of Trent*, trans. Rev. H. J. Schroeder, O.P. [Rockford, IL: TAN Books, 1978], Session 22, ch. 1, pp. 144–45). In other words, the Mass must continue as the Church's daily pleasing sacrifice to God, regardless of

what the external conditions may be. Prudence's role is not to cancel Mass or sacramental access, or to severely limit them, but to determine how best to ensure their unbroken *continuation* under the circumstances. There is a deeper theological perversion that explains the willingness to suspend sacraments, namely, the pervasive influence of a modernist account of sacraments as "salvation theater" in which we symbolically enact and thereby recall what has already objectively taken place in the "Christ-event"; in short, the sacraments do not *effect* our salvation but only remind us of a salvation already accomplished. Hence they are no more necessary than theater productions. For a full analysis, see Thomas Pink, "Vatican II and Crisis in the Theology of Baptism," published at *The Josias* on November 2, 5, and 8, 2018.

88 As Archbishop Carlo Maria Viganò says: "If you celebrate only the Tridentine Mass and preach sound doctrine without ever mentioning the Council, what can they ever do to you? Throw you out of your churches, perhaps, and then what? No one can ever prevent you from renewing the Holy Sacrifice, even if it is on a makeshift altar in a cellar or an attic, as the refractory priests did during the French Revolution, or as happens still today in China. And if they try to distance you, resist: canon law serves to guarantee the government of the Church in the pursuit of its primary purposes, not to demolish it. Let's stop fearing that the fault of the schism lies

with those who denounce it, and not, instead, with those who carry it out: the ones who are schismatics and heretics are those who wound and crucify the Mystical Body of Christ, not those who defend it by denouncing the executioners!" (*Voice in the Wilderness*, 203).

89 For example, we see today that the work of the SSPX clergy who soldiered on without official ecclesiastical approval or permission, laboring under canonical irregularities for decades, has slowly been vindicated, as Vatican policy toward them shifted from outright hostility to resigned tolerance to benevolent acceptance (though the exact situation on the ground varies a great deal from place to place). For details, see my article "Is It Ever Okay to Take Shelter in an SSPX Mass?," *OnePeterFive*, April 3, 2019. For other cases where papal decisions have been overturned and seeming disobedience vindicated, see Timothy Flanders, "Why the Term 'Extraordinary Form' is Wrong," *The Meaning of Catholic*, August 9, 2019. Flanders's linguistic argument has been confirmed (albeit with a totally contrary understanding of the realities) by Pope Francis's effective abolition of the terminology of "ordinary and extraordinary forms" of the Mass.

90 *From Benedict's Peace to Francis's War*, 67.

91 *From Benedict's Peace to Francis's War*, 330–31.

92 See Acts 5:40–42: "Calling in the apostles, after they had scourged them, they charged them that they should not speak at all in the name of Jesus; and they dismissed them. And

they indeed went from the presence of the council, rejoicing that they were accounted worthy to suffer reproach for the name of Jesus. And every day they ceased not in the temple, and from house to house, to teach and preach Christ Jesus."

93 See Bronwen McShea, "Bishops Unbound: The History behind Today's Crisis of Church Leadership," *First Things*, January 2019.

94 Indeed, if we are not careful we will slip into a pair of errors condemned by Pope Pius IX in the *Syllabus of Errors*: "Right consists in the material fact. All human duties are an empty word, and all human facts have the force of right" (59) and "The injustice of an act when successful inflicts no injury on the sanctity of right" (61). Massimo Viglione comments: "We must be *'pleasing not to men, but to God, who tests our hearts'* (1 Thess 2:4). Exactly! Therefore, whoever obeys men while being aware of facilitating evil and obstructing the Good, whoever they may be—including the ecclesiastical hierarchy, including the pope—in reality becomes an accomplice of evil, of lies, and of error. Whoever obeys in these conditions disobeys God. *'Because no slave is greater than his master'* (Mt 10:24)" (*From Benedict's Peace to Francis's War*, 110).

95 *The Great Betrayal: Thoughts on the Destruction of the Mass* (Waterloo, ON: Arouca Press, 2021), 71–72. By "the ecumenists" he means the members of the Consilium who wanted to make the New Mass as close to Protestant worship

and as acceptable to Protestants as possible. For some striking evidence along these lines, see Sharon Kabel, "Catholic fact check: Jean Guitton, Pope Paul VI, and the liturgical reforms," December 7, 2020, https://sharonkabel.com/post/guitton/.

96 See the article mentioned in note 77.

About the Author

Peter Kwasniewski holds a B.A. in Liberal Arts from Thomas Aquinas College and an M.A. and Ph.D. in Philosophy from the Catholic University of America, with a specialization in the thought of St. Thomas Aquinas. After teaching at the International Theological Institute in Austria, he joined the founding team of Wyoming Catholic College, where he taught theology, philosophy, music, and art history and directed the choir and schola until 2018. Today, he is a full-time writer and public speaker whose work is seen at websites and in periodicals such as *The New Liturgical Movement*, *OnePeterFive*, *Rorate Caeli*, *The Remnant*, *Catholic Family News*, and *Latin Mass Magazine*. Dr. Kwasniewski has published extensively in academic and popular venues on sacramental and liturgical theology, the history and aesthetics of music, Catholic Social Teaching, and issues in the contemporary Church. He has written or edited sixteen books, including most recently *From Benedict's Peace to Francis's War* (Angelico, 2021) and *Ministers of Christ: Recovering the Roles of Clergy and Laity in an Age of Confusion* (Crisis Publications, 2021). His work has been translated into at least eighteen languages. For more information, visit his website: www.peterkwasniewski.com.

Sophia Institute

Sophia Institute is a nonprofit institution that seeks to nurture the spiritual, moral, and cultural life of souls and to spread the Gospel of Christ in conformity with the authentic teachings of the Roman Catholic Church.

Sophia Institute Press fulfills this mission by offering translations, reprints, and new publications that afford readers a rich source of the enduring wisdom of mankind.

Sophia Institute also operates the popular online Catholic resource CatholicExchange.com. *Catholic Exchange* provides world news from a Catholic perspective as well as daily devotionals and articles that will help readers to grow in holiness and live a life consistent with the teachings of the Church.

In 2013, Sophia Institute launched Sophia Institute for Teachers to renew and rebuild Catholic culture through service to Catholic education. With the goal of nurturing the spiritual, moral, and cultural life of souls, and an abiding respect for the role and work of teachers, we strive to provide materials and programs that are at once enlightening to the mind and ennobling to the heart; faithful and complete, as well as useful and practical.

Sophia Institute gratefully recognizes the Solidarity Association for preserving and encouraging the growth of our apostolate over the course of many years. Without their generous and timely support, this book would not be in your hands.

www.SophiaInstitute.com
www.CatholicExchange.com
www.SophiaInstituteforTeachers.org